Contents

Acknowledgements

Agence France-Presse for the use of a photo by Andrea Merola of St Marks Square, Venice, which first appeared in *The Sunday Times* on 17 January 1999 © 1999, Agence France-Presse (1999, Times Newspapers). **Arriva Trains Northern on behalf of Railtrack plc** for the use of extracts from the timetable of the Leeds to Carlisle, Carlisle to Leeds timetable No. 36 © Railtrack plc. **Caroline Binch** for the use of a new illustration based on one in *Gregory Cool* by Caroline Binch © 2002, Caroline Binch, previously unpublished. **The Geographical Association** for the use of text on the Place du Général de Gaulle from *Montreuil Data: A European Place Study* coordinated by Don Garnan © 1995, The Geographical Association (1995, The GA). **The Guardian** for the use of text from an article 'Climber's tip top Mission' by Luke Harding which appeared in *The Guardian* on 12th April 2001 © 2001, *The Guardian*. **Frances Lincoln Ltd** for the use of an extract from *Gregory Cool* by Caroline Binch © 1994, Caroline Binch (1994, Frances Lincoln). **Los Angeles Times Syndicate International** for the use of an extract and one graphic from 'Quake shocks Seattle' by Patrick McMahon which appeared in *USA Today* newspapers © *USA Today*; graphic by Bob Laird. **The Met Office** for the use of weather forecasts, European temperatures and other information supplied by the Met Office and based on information from their website www.metoffice.com © Crown Copyright. **The Mid-Hants Watercress Line** for the use of their 2002 timetable and information leaflet © 2002, Mid-Hants Watercress Line. **John Murray Publishers Ltd** for the use of 'Inexpensive Progress' by John Betjeman from *John Betjeman: Collected Poems* © 1958, John Betjeman (1958, John Murray Publishers). **News International Syndication** for the use of an extract by John Follain and a graphic by Gary Cook, Jenny Preece and Ian Moores from the article 'All rise: Venetians are losing that sinking feeling' from *The Sunday Times* of 17th January 1999 © 1999, Times Newspapers. **Orion Books** for the use of two extracts from *The Everest Years* by Chris Bonnington © 1986, Chris Bonnington (1986, Weidenfeld and Nicolson). **Oxfam Publishing** for the use of two extracts from 'The Red Umbrella' by Valerie Lapthorne from *Stories from overseas* © 1980, Oxfam Publishing (1980 reprinted 1988, Malvern Oxfam); for the use of two extracts from 'Llamito: A story from Peru' by Anna Carling McVittie from *Stories from Overseas: Tales from Peru and El Salvador* © 1994, Oxfam Publishing (1994, Malvern Oxfam). **Oxford University Press** for the use of one extract of text, map and key entitled 'Arctic' from *The Oxford Children's Encyclopedia of our World* © 1999, OUP. **Peak District National Park Authority** for the use of text extracts and photographs from their tourist leaflet of 1997. Text © 1997, Peak District National Park Authority. Photographs © 1997, Mike Williams at info@peak-pictures.com **The Penguin Group (UK)** for the use of an extract from *Anna, Grandpa and the big storm* by Carla Stevens © 1982, Carla Stevens (1982, Viking); for the use of an extract from *The House That Moved* by David Rees © 1978, David Rees (1978, Penguin). **The Peters Fraser and Dunlop Group** for the use of an extract from *Sinking Sands* by Anthony Masters © 1996, Anthony Masters (1996, Ginn and Company). **RNLI Sea Safety Liaison Working Group** for the use of extracts and illustrations from *Beach safety guidelines: safety on the sea* © RNLI. **The Random House Group** for the use of 'The café dog' from *The Beach Dogs* by Colin Dann © 1988, Colin Dann (1988, Hutchinson, Beaver Books). **Anita Marie Sackett** for the use of 'A tapestry of sounds' © 2002, Anita Marie Sackett, previously unpublished. **Scholastic Inc, New York** for the use of text and illustrations from *The Magic School Bus Inside the Earth* by Joanna Cole, illustrated by Bruce Degan. Text © 1987, Joanna Cole, illustrations © 1987, Bruce Degan (The Magic School Bus is a registered trademark of Scholastic Inc). **Silva Limited** for the use of images and text from the Silva compass leaflet © Silva Ltd. **The United Kingdom Hydrographic Office** for the use of tidal information reproduced by permission of the Controller of Her Majesty's Stationery Office and the UK Hydrographic Office © UKHO (www.ukho.gov.uk). **Usborne Publishing Ltd** for the use of illustrations and text entitled 'Where does water come from?' from *Finding out about our earth* by Jane Chisholm © 1982, Usborne Publishing.

Every effort has been made to trace copyright holders and the publishers apologise for any omissions.

Geography
ages 7–11

Stuart May, Paula Richardson & Emma Till

Clarendon Avenue,
Leamington Spa,
Warwickshire
CV32 5PR
www.scholastic.co.uk

Printed by Bell & Bain Ltd, Glasgow
Text © 2002 Stuart May, Paula Richardson and Emma Till
© 2002 Scholastic Ltd
1 2 3 4 5 6 7 8 9 0   2 3 4 5 6 7 8 9 0 1

Authors

Stuart May, Paula Richardson and Emma Till

Editor

Christine Harvey

Assistant Editor

Dulcie Booth

Series designer

Lynne Joesbury

Designer

Paul Cheshire

Illustrations

Sarah Warburton

Cover illustration

Jon Berkeley

British Library Cataloguing-in-Publication Data
A catalogue record for this book is available from the British Library.

ISBN 0-439-98312-6

Designed using Adobe Pagemaker

Introduction

We cannot escape from geography. It constantly surrounds us – when we go on holiday, when we watch the news on television. It is a part of children's lives from the moment they begin to take an intelligent interest in the world around them. By the time they begin their formal schooling, children have a wide, but disorganised, awareness of the world, including the world beyond their immediate, first-hand experience. During Key Stage 1, their geographical experience is widened and they begin to acquire a framework of knowledge of the world into which their learning and experiences can be fitted.

At Key Stage 2, while continuing their study of places as they did at Key Stage 1, children will also study some geographical themes, such as settlements, and aspects of weather and climate, either through their place studies or through a continuing study unit. They will complement these physical and human geography units with the study of an environmental issue. All these areas of learning can be supplemented and developed through the use of this book. It is designed to help children develop their skills of interpreting and using a variety of sources of information.

The texts selected for this book reflect the authors' belief that literacy involves not only the ability to read and understand text, but to obtain and evaluate material from a range of sources in order to broaden experiences and develop knowledge. The texts here have been chosen for their contribution to geographical understanding, and for their variety. It is our aim that they be interesting as well as informative, so that they encourage children to find out more; to continue or extend the reading and geographical research that they initiate.

We have also interpreted the term 'text' liberally. The extracts in the book range from annotated maps and diagrams, brochures and posters, to traditional texts, both fiction and non-fiction.

There are many ways of using the texts in this book to link in with the geographical learning of your class. Even though the chapters are themed (for ease of use and reference), many of the texts can be used to contribute to other areas of the geography curriculum.

It is important to draw out specific points in the texts to bring out underlying geographical issues. Similarly, where a text exemplifies a process, such as the water cycle, look at more specific examples, such as how this relates to your own area.

Teaching geography through texts

Geography is too big a subject to expect to study all of it at first hand. First-hand experience, through fieldwork, is essential for children throughout Key Stage 2, but much of their geographical studies will rely on the use of secondary sources – many of which will be text-based. These texts will take a variety of forms, from labels and captions to notes and sustained writing. Text will also reflect the society from which it comes, either through the language or alphabet used, or through its cultural references – or a combination of both these.

The texts included here support an enquiry approach to geographical learning. Children should be encouraged to both ask questions and consider where and how they might find answers. The texts can either be used to provide information, or as a stimulus. In either case, children should be encouraged to pose questions in response to the texts, to find out more about what is in them or to question them – considering a text's standpoint, bias or usefulness in a specific context. In other words, as well as being inquisitive, the children should be critical.

The National Literacy Strategy

Although chosen for their geographical content, the texts in this book are designed to fit in with the National Literacy Strategy. They offer:

◆ a variety of genres
◆ extracts from stories
◆ a range of vocabulary related to the subject matter
◆ word-, sentence- and text-level work
◆ opportunities for prediction and reflection
◆ opportunities for discussion, and developing speaking and listening skills, as well as critical thinking.

Teaching with text and ICT

There are a variety of opportunities within this book to integrate the work undertaken with ICT. Use a selection of the following activities to develop the use of ICT with your class:

◆ writing stories, individually or cooperatively, over time or in one session
◆ making and labelling maps, diagrams, graphs and charts (using drawing programs)
◆ writing labels
◆ writing descriptions to compare with texts
◆ reordering text
◆ giving and following directions, and using maps on screen
◆ producing brochures or reports (using a simple desktop publishing program)
◆ sequencing text and producing a simple map from this
◆ researching information (using the Internet).

Finally, you will come up with your own ideas for using the texts in this book as you get to know it more. The important thing to remember is that this book is designed to develop geographical knowledge, skills and understanding through the use of texts. The more children are able to use texts properly and critically, the better they will be able to learn in any subject, but the more they enjoy texts, the more they will want to learn. Never work on a text with the children so much that it takes this enjoyment away. Let the story, especially, come through.

EXTRACT	GENRE	GEOGRAPHY LEARNING OBJECTIVES	LITERACY LEARNING OBJECTIVES	PAGE
Places				
World environments	Reference/information text	1a, 1c, 2c, 3a, 3g	◆ To define terms. ◆ To change verb tenses. ◆ To investigate plurals.	10
A tapestry of sounds	Story from another culture	1a, 2a, 2c, 3a–c, 3f, 6b	◆ To understand the use of commas. ◆ To produce creative writing in a given setting. ◆ To use sounds for poetic effect.	14
Montreuil	Information in the form of a table	1a, 1b, 1c, 2a, 2c, 2e, 3c, 3g	◆ To develop unfamiliar vocabulary. ◆ To investigate roots of words. ◆ To interpret tabulated data.	17
Llamito	Story from another culture	1b, 1e, 2c, 2f, 3a, 3g	◆ To predict the setting of a story. ◆ To investigate the portrayal of characters. ◆ To summarise text.	21
Gregory Cool	Story from another culture	1b, 1c, 2b, 2c, 2d, 3a, 3b, 3g, 6b	◆ To investigate different styles of speech and language. ◆ To discuss the importance of setting to a story. ◆ To develop understanding of syllables.	24
The house on stilts	Story in an unfamiliar setting	1a, 1c, 2d, 5a	◆ To use specialist vocabulary. ◆ To investigate the creative use of words. ◆ To develop report-writing skills.	27
Peak National Park	Brochure and reference text	2c, 2d, 3a–c, 4b, 5a, 5b, 6d	◆ To discuss the importance of text layout. ◆ To investigate writing newspaper articles. ◆ To formulate questions based on information.	30
The Arctic	Non-fiction text	1b, 1c, 2c, 2d, 2f, 3a–c, 3g, 7b	◆ To consider different types of writing. ◆ To develop understanding of the use of dashes. ◆ To use appropriate language to create dramatic description.	34
Physical geography				
Sinking sands	Adventure story in a familiar setting	1a, 1e, 2g, 4a, 4b, 6c	◆ To predict the outcome of a story. ◆ To develop the use of adjectives. ◆ To investigate long vowel patterns.	38
Inside the earth	Information text	1a, 1b, 2d, 4b	◆ To investigate syllables. ◆ To compare US/UK English. ◆ To understand the use of possessive apostrophes.	41
Weather forecast	Information text, tables and map	1a, 1b, 1c, 1e, 2d, 2f, 4b	◆ To use information displayed in a variety of ways. ◆ To identify appropriate language for different audiences. ◆ To investigate writing a script.	45
Checks by the sea	Information/instructions in the form of a poster	2d, 3d, 3f, 4a, 4b, 6c	◆ To analyse information on a poster. ◆ To investigate contractions. ◆ To distinguish between fact and opinion.	49
Preparing for an earthquake	Information/instructions	2d, 2g, 4b	◆ To recognise and follow written instructions. ◆ To prepare and carry out an interview. ◆ To investigate diary writing style.	52
Quake shocks Seattle	Newspaper report	1c, 2a, 2d, 3e, 4b	◆ To investigate styles of newspaper articles. ◆ To consider the use of emotive words and phrases. ◆ To devise interview questions.	55
Anna, Grandpa and the big storm	Story in a familiar setting	2c, 2d, 3d, 4b	◆ To investigate how people react within their character. ◆ To develop use of synonyms. ◆ To focus on suffixes.	58
Where does water come from?	Information text – illustration and labels	1b, 2g, 4b, 6e	◆ To retrieve information from text. ◆ To sequence text in a specific order. ◆ To identify differences between fact and fiction.	61
Water's progress	Information text – diagram and captions	2a, 2c, 2d, 4a, 4b, 6c	◆ To investigate the use of information material. ◆ To recognise comparative and superlative adjectives. ◆ To identify compound words.	64
The river's song	Poem	1b, 2a, 2c, 3e, 3g	◆ To investigate the use of pattern in poetry. ◆ To identify alliteration and its use. ◆ To explore rhyming words.	67
Human geography				
What's in a name?	Information text	1b, 1c, 2c, 3a, 3c, 4a, 4b, 6d	◆ To discuss the origins of words. ◆ To investigate the pronunciation of words. ◆ To write a story set in a specific place.	71
Europa	Information text in a persuasive leaflet/travel brochure	1d, 2a, 2c, 3a, 3c, 3d, 3f, 3g, 7b	◆ To investigate the use of persuasive vocabulary. ◆ To identify the use and impact of different fonts and typesizes. ◆ To understand the difference between common and proper nouns.	74

EXTRACT	GENRE	GEOGRAPHY LEARNING OBJECTIVES	LITERACY LEARNING OBJECTIVES	PAGE
The café dog	Fictional extract from a longer story/novel	1b, 1c, 2d, 3a, 3f, 6d	◆ To continue a story. ◆ To write an account in the first person. ◆ To compare the same author's style in different books.	78
The Red Umbrella – Part One	Story from another culture	1a, 1c, 1d, 3a, 3f, 6b	◆ To understand how to represent speech in writing. ◆ To use rhythm in poetry. ◆ To use a variety of adjectives.	81
The Red Umbrella – Part Two	Story from another culture	1a, 1c, 2b, 3a, 6b, 7a	◆ To deduce word meaning from its context. ◆ To write sequential instructions. ◆ To develop arguments for and against a proposition.	84
Town transect	Diagram with labels	1b, 1c, 2a, 3e, 3f, 6a, 7c	◆ To investigate explanatory captions. ◆ To compile a glossary. ◆ To create full sentences from captions.	87
Town and country	Information text – illustrations and captions	1b, 2a, 2c, 3a, 3b	◆ To write using persuasive language. ◆ To investigate alternative names for features. ◆ To answer comprehension questions on a text.	90

Environmental geography

EXTRACT	GENRE	GEOGRAPHY LEARNING OBJECTIVES	LITERACY LEARNING OBJECTIVES	PAGE
Inexpensive progress	Poem	1b, 1d, 3a, 3e, 4a, 5a	◆ To discuss rhyming patterns. ◆ To write a short review of a poem. ◆ To identify and discuss others' points of view.	95
Skylines	Illustrations, and extracts from classic fiction and poetry	1a, 1c, 2b, 3a, 3c, 3e, 6d, 6e	◆ To discuss the use of descriptive language to create a picture. ◆ To rewrite text in a contrasting style. ◆ To investigate words with multiple meanings.	98
Everest	Newspaper article and autobiography	1a, 1c, 2c, 2f, 3b, 5a, 5b	◆ To discuss text in terms of fact and opinion. ◆ To investigate different writing styles. ◆ To research and write an article.	102
All rise	Newspaper article	1a, 1c, 1d, 3a, 3b, 3c, 4b, 5a, 5b	◆ To write a story in a given setting. ◆ To develop character profiles. ◆ To investigate the use of technical language.	106
Survey on pollution	Questionnaire	1a, 1b, 1c, 2b, 2f, 3e, 4b, 5a, 5b	◆ To investigate leading questions. ◆ To identify words which ask questions. ◆ To revise question marks.	109
The house that moved	Text that raises an issue	1b, 1c, 2b, 2f, 3a–d, 4a, 5a, 5b	◆ To predict story plots. ◆ To discuss 'poetic licence'. ◆ To develop letter-writing skills.	112

Geographical skills

EXTRACT	GENRE	GEOGRAPHY LEARNING OBJECTIVES	LITERACY LEARNING OBJECTIVES	PAGE
Colours in our landscape	Non-fiction information text	1a, 1b, 2b, 2d, 4a	◆ To develop plans for stories. ◆ To devise questions for further investigation. ◆ To investigate idioms.	116
Paragon hotel	Information text and map	1a, 2a, 2c, 2d, 3b, 3c, 3g, 7b	◆ To practise formal letter writing. ◆ To investigate the layout of addresses. ◆ To look at verb tenses.	119
The Watercress Line	Information/persuasive leaflet	1a, 1b, 1c, 1d, 2c, 2d, 4a, 7a	◆ To analyse the format of a leaflet/brochure. ◆ To rewrite text for a different audience. ◆ To identify different punctuation marks.	123
Read this, or get lost	Procedural and information text within a publicity brochure (with persuasive elements)	1a, 2a, 2b, 2g, 3g	◆ To discuss the style of advertising and procedural text. ◆ To produce instructions/procedural writing. ◆ To design slogans.	127
For sale	Advertisement and information text	1a, 1b, 2a, 2d, 2g, 4a	◆ To investigate the use of abbreviations. ◆ To discuss the use of persuasive language. ◆ To differentiate between vowels and consonants.	132
Train timetable	Timetable and notes	1b, 1c, 2c, 2d, 3a–c	◆ To understand timetables and explanatory notes. ◆ To use proper nouns. ◆ To develop a story around places in a timetable.	135
Geographical dictionary	Information text/ dictionary	1a, 1b, 2a, 2d, 4a, 4b	◆ To discuss subject-specific language. ◆ To identify a range of reference resources. ◆ To practise segmenting words into phonemes.	139
Make a visitor's guide	Instructions	1a, 1b, 1c, 1e, 7c	◆ To understand the features of instructional writing. ◆ To design a brochure. ◆ To turn prose into bullet-pointed lists.	142

Places

The study of places is central to geographical studies at Key Stage 2. Children learn about other places around the world and how they can be compared with their own. Studying places occupies such a central position because it brings together all aspects of geographical study into one whole concept – the concept of 'place' as a unique experience.

As geographers, we ask, *What is this place like?* In answering this question, we can investigate what makes the place as it is, how it has become like that (how it has developed over time) and how it is linked to other places.

In investigating places, children will begin to understand how and why areas are as they are, as well as understanding some of the similarities and differences between them, and why the way people live their lives differs around the world.

Place studies also provides a starting point for the other aspects of Key Stage 2 geographical study – physical, human and environmental geography. These concentrate on some of the common processes and patterns that are apparent between places, and although they are more concerned with the processes themselves, the examples and case studies are drawn from the real world – from *places*.

The selected texts in this chapter illustrate aspects of life in Africa, Asia, the Caribbean, Europe and the UK. The final text encourages research into life in the Arctic.

World environments

Genre
reference/
information
text

Coniferous forest
These are found in northern, cold environments. Most of the trees are evergreens, such as pine and yew trees. Wild animals, such as wolves, bears and foxes, live in these areas.

Savanna
Grasslands in hot areas are called savanna. This is where elephants, giraffes, lions and rhinoceros live, grazing on the tall grasses and leaves of the acacia trees that grow here.

Woodland
These areas can consist of deciduous trees, such as oak and hazel, in Britain, and acacia and eucalyptus forests in Australia. Woodland animals include parrots, wood pigeons and squirrels.

Tundra
This is flat land with no trees. Vegetation comprises lichens, mosses and grasses that grow above the soil, which is frozen for most of the year. Animals that can withstand the cold, such as voles, lemmings, and Arctic foxes, live in this environment all the time. Birds and reindeer live there in the warmer summer months when the ground thaws.

Desert
These are dry expanses of land, that have hardly any rainfall. The environment consists of sand, gravel and big rocks. Scrubland and cacti are the only vegetation. Many animals that live in the desert are nocturnal, as the land is hot by day and cooler at night. These animals include snakes and lizards.

Mediterranean woodland

This region has short winters and hot, dry summers. Vegetation is largely evergreen trees and shrubs, such as lavender and olive trees. Lizards, rodents, bats and birds live in this environment.

 Tropical rainforest

This environment has the same weather throughout the year, always hot and humid with constant rain. Vegetation is diverse and grows in layers, with a high canopy of large trees, smaller trees below this, and shrubs on ground level. Different animals live in the layers, including monkeys, macaws, frogs and snakes.

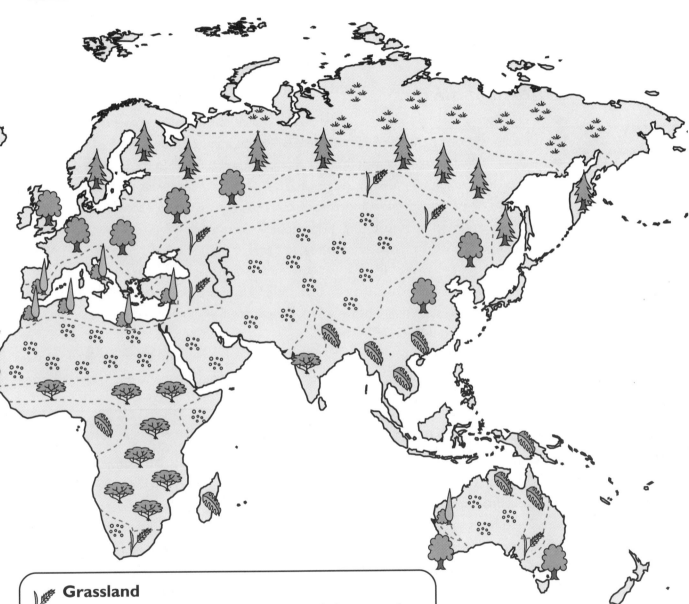

Grassland

These environments have many animals living in them as grass is a good food source. Grasslands in Australia have kangaroos, emus and wild horses living on them. There is also a great variety of insects, such as beetles and earthworms in the soil and on the plants.

© Geoatlas

World environments

Geography learning objectives

◆ To ask geographical questions (1a).

◆ To analyse evidence and draw conclusions (1c).

◆ To use atlases and globes (2c).

◆ To identify and describe what places are like (3a).

◆ To recognise how places fit within a wider geographical context (3g).

Vocabulary

Environment, desert, cacti, scrubland, tundra, arctic, reindeer, lichens, grassland, kangaroo, savanna, giraffes, coniferous, evergreens, vegetation, nocturnal.

Discussing the text

◆ Read the title of the text with the children and ask them to predict the contents. Ask them how they think it might be set out, and whether there will be diagrams or prose.

◆ Read out each of the environment titles, for example *desert* and *grassland*. Challenge the children to define each of the terms by asking questions, such as *What is a desert environment like? What sort of features would you expect to see in a tropical rainforest?* Then give each child a copy of the text and to compare the definitions there with the children's definitions. What things did they know before reading the text, and what information was new to them?

◆ Discuss the overall layout of the text with the children and talk about it in terms of other non-fiction texts they have come across. Do they think the information is clearly set out? Are the headings effective? Ask them to suggest alternative ways of presenting the information, drawing on what the children have seen in other non-fiction texts.

◆ Do the children think it is easy to identify the different environments on the map? Make sure they are clear about which part of the world each environment is in and use this to encourage discussion on world places.

Geography activities

◆ Ask the children to form small groups and allocate each group one of the environments in the text to work on. Get them to create a picture to illustrate the description provided. They will need to think about how to interpret the description and think about how to create a realistic picture of the place. These can then be annotated and displayed. Discuss the results with the whole class. Did they have an image in their minds or did they have to rely on the words in the text? How clear was the written description? What other words would have helped?

◆ Ask the children to identify countries and towns which fall into the category of each of the environments given in the text, and to record these, both on the map and on a chart, for example, East Africa has savanna areas. They can find climatic data, either in a reference book or on the Internet, and plot this on a graph. After identifying the main features of each environment, ask them to write a brief description of each one. If possible, encourage them to use actual data in the description.

◆ Involve the children in some detailed comparative work using the text and a good atlas or map. Ask them to focus on countries in a particular climate zone, for example California, southern European countries, parts of Australia and South Africa. They can mark and label these on the map after identifying their position in the atlas.

◆ Take a particular country, such as Australia, and get the children to identify all the climatic variations which can be found there. Encourage them to use physical and human maps of Australia, and to match them up with a climatic map. Then ask questions, such as *What effect does high land have on the vegetation of a particular area? What is the impact on climate and population in the very middle of Australia? Why are there so many towns on the coast of Australia?*

◆ Ask the children to identify all the main deserts in the world and label them on the map in the text. Look at some pictures of desert scenes with them and ask what they think deserts were used for in the past. (For camel treks, rearing goats, growing dates and crops at an oasis.) How are they used now? (For oil, exploration, tourism.) Ask the children if cold places can be deserts too.

Further literacy ideas

◆ Ask the children to choose one of the environments in the text, such as tundra, and make up a glossary or dictionary for the geographical terms in the information, such as *arctic, mosses, lichens, voles, reindeer.*

◆ The children can choose an environment from the text in which to set a story. Ask them to use information from the text to add detail to the description of the setting, for example a story set in a tropical rainforest should make reference to the vegetation and the wildlife, such as monkeys and snakes.

◆ Ask the children to choose another subject similar to the text, such as world rainfall or world temperatures, and to use the text as a model to make their own version of it. Point out that it should be non-chronological, have sub-headings, text boxes or a key.

◆ Use some of the animal names in the text to revise the spelling of plurals. Give the children a list of singular versions of the words, such as *bear, fox* and *wolf* and ask them to rewrite the word in its plural form, or vice versa.

◆ Ask the children to experiment with changing some of the tenses in this text and discuss its impact on the style of this explanatory text.

◆ Look at connectives in a guided session with the class. Some of the text on the environments contains a series of short sentences, for example the coniferous forests. Ask the children to rewrite the information on one of the environments using one or more connectives, for example *These are found in northern, cold environments **and** most of the trees are evergreens.*

◆ Use some of the writing in the text to revise the use of commas when listing, for example *Grasslands in Australia have kangaroos, emus and wild horses.*

Genre
story from another culture

A tapestry of sounds

The market is alive with the hubbub of buying and selling. A tapestry of sounds.

"Come, come. Look, buy."

Veiled women in dark robes swish past stalls of pomegranates, potatoes, sugarcane and spices.

Donkeys pull laden carts, clattering over cobbles, whilst klaxons blare above the cobblers' tap, tapping and the whirr, whirr of tailors' sewing machines.

Waiting camels spit, caged canaries sing, tourists haggle and a beggar rattles his tin.

Anita Marie Sackett

A tapestry of sounds

Geography learning objectives

◆ To ask geographical questions and use geographical vocabulary (1a, 2a).

◆ To use atlases and maps to identify, locate and describe what Cairo is like (2c, 3a–c).

◆ To make observations about life in Cairo (3a, 3f).

◆ To describe how Cairo is similar to and different to a know locality (3f).

◆ To look at a place that is less economically developed (6b).

Background notes

The story is set in Cairo and provides an opportunity to introduce a distant and very different locality to the children. It would also provide a link with any history study of Ancient Egypt.

Vocabulary

Sounds, donkeys, camels, hubbub, whistle, tapestry, pomegranates, whirr, archway, carts, klaxons.

Discussing the text

◆ Ask the children to focus on the text without looking at the illustration. Read the text through with them and ask where they think the story is set. What evidence is there in the text to support their ideas? (Camels, veiled women.)

◆ Talk with the children about the narrative voice in the story. What person is the narrative written in? Ask the children to support their answers with examples from the text.

◆ Ask the children about the phrase *cobblers' tap, tapping and the whirr, whirr of tailors' sewing machines.* Do the children think these are effective ways of describing the sounds? They could be asked to choose a percussion instrument that they think reflects the sounds that the cobblers or the tailors make, or suggest an alternative way of describing the noises.

◆ Talk about the market place with the children – the goods on sale there, and the people and animals described. Do they think the writing is successful at depicting the environment of the market?

◆ Talk about the picture with the children. How does it enhance the story? Does it tell them more than the text? Discuss what is going on in the picture, focusing on the sounds and smells that might be there.

Geography activities

◆ Discuss with the children what the place in the illustration is like. Focus their attention on what the buildings and streets are like. Can they find examples of interesting window shapes, for instance? What do they notice about the transport?

◆ Find Cairo on a map with the class and ask the children a series of questions about it. *In which country/continent is it? How could you travel there? Which countries would you travel over to get there if you travelled by air and also over land? What are its neighbouring countries and cities?* Then, using atlases, ask the children to find out how far Cairo is from some capital cities, such as London, New York, Baghdad, New Delhi.

◆ Use some pictures of modern Cairo to show the differences between old and new Cairo. Ask the children to identify these differences. What has remained the same?

◆ Ask the children to look at the market. What are the features that tell them it's a market? Ask them what the advantages of selling in a market are (lower overheads, easy to change commodities and prices as needed). Ask them to draw a picture of the Cairo market and one of a market known to them, labelling as many features as they can, and identifying the differences and similarities.

◆ What kind of jobs can the children identify in the illustration? Ask them to look at how people are dressed and to suggest why this is so. Who do they think might buy the goods on sale both in the market and the shops? (Get them to think about the goods and services on sale and to connect these to people's needs.)

◆ Using travel brochures, ask the children to work out the cost of a holiday to Cairo. What would they want to see and do there, and how might these activities affect the price? Encourage them to look up the daily temperatures and weather for Cairo on an Internet site. Then make a display entitled 'Planning my holiday to Cairo'.

Further literacy ideas

◆ Use the text as a basis for looking at comma usage in sentences with the children. Ask them to read the text to a partner leaving out the commas, and then discuss the effect of this. Give the children the text, or a similar piece of prose, without commas, and ask them to put the commas in the correct places.

◆ Ask the children to write a story entitled 'The Market in Cairo'. Tell them to use the same setting as in the text and to use the picture to give them ideas. Give the children a story planner first. To ensure they capture the mood and atmosphere of the market, brainstorm suitable words they could use before they start writing.

◆ Ask the children to write a poem entitled 'Sounds'. Use the title of the text as a starting point, discussing the weaving together of sounds to create a tapestry. This activity could be done as a shared or guided writing lesson with the children, suggesting sounds and modelling how to collate the ideas into the format of a poem.

◆ Discuss the use of sound in writing to create poetic effects, such as alliteration and onomatopoeia. Ask the children to identify examples of these effects in the text.

Montreuil

Building use in Place du Général de Gaulle

Genre
information
in the form of
a table

Building number	Use
1 & 3	Electrical shop
2	Toy novelties
4	Masseur – alternative medicine
5	Insurance office
6	Electrical repairs
7	Café
8	Video shop
9	Sports shop
10	Empty
11	Empty
12	Private house
13	Butcher
14	Doctor's surgery and take-away shop
15	Insurance office
16	Private house
17 & 19	Closed bar and restaurant
18	Funeral parlour
20	Private house
21	Bar Chevaux d'Or
22	Private house
23	Bar le Diplomate
24	Private house
25	Wedding gown shop
26	Private house
27	Private house
28	Baker
29 & 31	Shoe shop

Building number	Use
30	Empty
32	Bar/hotel – Theatre
33	Private house
34	Bank (Crédit Agricole)
35	Bank (Crédit du Nord)
36	Men's hairdresser
37	Private house
38	Post Office (photographic studio)
39	Private house
40	Private house
41 & 43	Hardware shop
42 & 44	Clothes store
45	Chemist/pharmacy
46	Supermarket
47	Tea room/private house
48	Restaurant/hotel
49	Jewellery shop
50	Restaurant/hotel
51	Insurance office
52	Pizza café
53	Co-op Agricole offices
54	Book shop
55	Driving school
56	Toys
57	Flower shop
58	Grocer/wine shop
59	Barber (men)
60	Vet's surgery

Goods sold from market stalls in Place du Général de Gaulle

Stall number	Use
1	Flowers
2	Meat
3	Cooked meats
4	Cooked meats
5	Vegetables
6	Roast chickens
7	Fruit
8	Vegetables
9	Fruit and farm produce
10	Meat
11	Vegetables
12	Vegetables/plants
13	Flowers, vegetables/fruit (artichokes, Brussels sprouts, endive, avocado, peppers, garlic, kiwi fruit, strawberries)
14	Meat
15	Farm produce
16	Vegetables
17	Clothes (men)
18	Clothes
19	Clothes (ladies: nearly new)
20	Plants
21	Clothes
22	Jewellery-novelties
23	Clothes
24	Curtain materials
25	Leather goods

Stall number	Use
26	Sweets
27	Shoes
28	Toys/baskets/cushions
29	Leather bags
30	Bedding/towels
31	Novelties, belts, necklaces
32	Clothes, woollens, etc
33	Clothes (children's)
34	Shoes
35	Clothes (woollens)
36	Clothes (ladies)
37	Toiletries
38	Clothes (ladies' nightclothes)
39	Clothes (shirts)
40	Material
41	Clothes (ladies)
42	Clothes (ladies' dresses)
43	Scarves
44	Curtain materials
45	Belts
46	Baskets
47	Woollens
48	Haberdashery, clothes, threads, etc
49	Kitchen utensils, garden equipment
50	Footballs
51	Clothes (second-hand ladies' dresses)

ontreuil

Geography learning objectives

◆ To ask geographical questions and use appropriate geographical vocabulary (1a, 2a).

◆ To collect and record evidence, and draw plans (1b, 2e).

◆ To analyse evidence and draw conclusions (1c).

◆ To use atlases, maps and pictures (2c).

◆ To describe where places are (3c).

◆ To recognise how Montreuil fits into a wider geographical context (3g).

Background notes

This extract helps to develop the children's knowledge and concepts of a European place. For some schools who visit northern France in the upper primary school it could provide material for a fieldwork exercise.

Vocabulary

Building, electrical, medicine, insurance, empty, private, butcher, restaurant, pharmacy, theatre, jewellery, flower, grocer, livestock, vegetables, strawberries, cushions, haberdashery, utensils.

Discussing the text

◆ Show the children the title of the first piece of text on an OHP. Does this give them any clues as to what the text might be about? Do they know what country it is from? Do they think it will be a fiction or non-fiction piece of text? Discuss the language of the text – what language do the children think the text will be written in and why do they think this?

◆ Reveal the first two columns of text to the children. Read through the text with them and discuss the pronunciation and meaning of any unfamiliar vocabulary, such as *masseur*. Challenge the children to suggest what the *Bar Chevaux d'Or* might be. Show them how to use other known words from their own language to help them work out the meaning of the text, for example use the word *Bar Le Diplomate* and their knowledge of the English word *bar* to find a meaning.

◆ Look at the second column of text with the class and discuss the words where there are French and English together, for example *Bank (Crédit Agricole)*. Can the children identify any links between the words used and their meaning? (For instance, point out the meaning of the word *credit* and how it would be linked to a bank.)

◆ Ask the children to look at the second piece of text and discuss any unknown vocabulary with them, such as *artichokes*, *endive*, *haberdashery*.

◆ What type of book do the children think these extracts have come from? Who do the children think the intended audience is? (Explain that they're from an educational information pack.)

Geography activities

◆ Discuss with the children where they think the 'market stalls' in the text are located. What are the clues? (The title.) Ask them to look at the lists in each shopping area and to identify the main groups the goods fall into (clothing, food, services). The children can graph the results and comment on them.

◆ Ask the children to debate what size Montreuil might be. Is it a village, town or city? Ask them to account for their answers. Using an atlas, get them to locate Montreuil. How far is it from the ports of Calais or Boulogne? Give out road atlases of France so that they can locate the town more accurately. What are the surrounding towns called? How could they travel there from school?

◆ Ask the children how shops and services differ in a town and a city. Give them a list of services, such as a multiplex cinema, a small cinema, a department store, a large hospital, council offices, and ask them to identify which would be found in a town or a city. Why do they think that big department stores are generally only found in large towns or cities? (They need a large number of people to visit to ensure sales.) Ask them to think of services and shops around them which are in towns and cities.

◆ Look at the shops in the 'Place du Général de Gaulle' in the texts with the class. Using other pictures of a French towns, discuss the layout of their central squares, with its open central market area, town hall, cafés, statues. Look at the way the houses and shops are shown often with shutters, flower baskets and names above the doors. Ask the children to draw a plan to show the possible layout of the square in Montreuil, using the information from the text and the evidence of the pictures they have looked at.

◆ Why do the children think the square was named 'Place du Général de Gaulle'? Ask the children to do some research on Général de Gaulle. Who was he and why was he so famous? Ask them to think about the streets in their area. Are there any interesting names which commemorate people and events in history? (Victoria Street, Churchill Way.) Use a street map of the local area and ask the children to research street names and to tie them to people and events where possible. Write to the planning department of the local town council and ask them about the methods they use to determine names of new streets in the area.

◆ Introduce the children to other places in France through the use of an atlas and road atlas. Ask: *How large is France in comparison to Britain? Which are the main towns and cities?* Using the scale of the map, ask them to work out distances between places in France, for instance how far is it from Paris to Nice? Ask them to work out other places and countries in the same latitude as Paris and Nice. Then ask them to look at places in Britain and work out how far it is from Newcastle to London, for example. Which places in Scandinavia are in the same latitude as Hull, Newcastle or Aberdeen? This sort of information comes as a surprise to children and helps them to recognise that other European places are not as remote as they might have thought.

Further literacy ideas

◆ Give the children a column of words from the text, or just a selection, and ask them to sort them alphabetically. Ensure that there are a number of words that will require the children to look at the second, and where possible, third letter of the word in order to arrange them correctly.

◆ In a guided writing lesson, show the children how words are often created from one root word, for example *novelty* comes from the root *novel*. Ask the children to identify other root words in the texts and to explore their meanings.

◆ Get the children to write a story entitled 'Lost', which centres on them becoming detached from their friends, family or school party when visiting France, or another country.

◆ Ask the children to pretend to be one of the shop owners in the 'building' text, and to write to the council about their concerns over the number of empty properties in Montreuil. Discuss with the children the points that they might want to make to the council, such as the effect on passing trade or the litter created.

Llamito

Genre
story from
another
culture

Maria Luisa and her family live in a small village in Peru, high in the Andes mountains, near the town of Cusco. The little houses are clustered together on rough grassland. There are a few trees, but nobody has a flower garden. The houses have thatched roofs, and the walls are of bricks made from mud, stone and straw or tough grasses. Maria Luisa's father built their house himself, mixing the bricks, putting them in moulds, and then drying them in the sun.

It's a good house, keeping the family dry and sheltered in the wet weather, and protecting them from the heat of the sun in dry weather. From the window, Maria Luisa can look across the valley and see craggy snow-capped mountain peaks in the distance. All the family live in one large room: Maria Luisa's father and mother, Cesar and Margarita Quispe; her little brother, Jose; and their elderly grand-parents, Abuela and Abuelo. They have two dogs, Mo and To, two oxen, and a llama named Ernestina. Although Maria Luisa, her parents, brother and grand-parents live so closely together, there are few quarrels, for in Peru families are very united and look after one another. They all share the work, and nobody need ever feel lonely.

On one particular morning, as Abuela was putting Maria Luisa's black hair into the two long plaits that the womenfolk of her people traditionally wear, Papa Cesar came rushing into the house, clapping his hands and laughing.

"I am sure of it," he cried, "absolutely sure! Ernestina is going to have a baby!"

This first birth would be of great importance to them. Llamas (which are related to camels) are used for carrying loads; their thick wool is used for weaving; their meat is sometimes eaten and their milk is drunk. These animals provide the main way in which many mountain families in Peru earn their living. So, as this news about Ernestina was an occasion to celebrate, Mama Margarita and Abuela promised they would make a very special supper that evening, and said they would invite their relations and friends who lived near to join them.

Anna Carling McVittie

Llamito

Geography learning objectives

◆ To collect and record evidence (1b).

◆ To communicate in a variety of ways (1e).

◆ To use atlases and globes (2c).

◆ To use ICT to help in geographical investigations (2f).

◆ To identify and describe what places are like (3a).

◆ To recognise how places fit within a wider geographical context (3g).

Background notes

This is an extract from a traditional story from Peru and provides an opportunity to look more generally at the continent of South America, as well as the country of Peru.

Vocabulary

Peru, Andes mountains, clustered, thatched roofs, craggy, llama, plaits, traditional.

Discussing the text

◆ Read the text through with the class and ask them where they think the story is set. What clues are there in the text to support their suggestions? Make a list with the children of all the clues that give information about the setting (the description of the houses, weather references and the mention of the snow-capped mountains).

◆ Do any of the children know where Peru is? Talk about the location of Peru in relation to the UK.

◆ Discuss the word *llama*. Do the children know how to pronounce this word? Have they ever seen a llama? Do any of them know what a llama looks like? Explain their main characteristics to the children and show them some pictures.

◆ Read the text to the end of paragraph four. Do the children know who, or what, Ernestina is? (Although the passage does mention briefly that she is a llama, this is quite easy to miss.) Talk about the skill of 'skim reading', but also how sometimes it is important to read the text slowly.

◆ Talk about the names of the characters in this story. Have the children heard of any of these names before? What do names tell us about the setting of a story? Can the children think of other stories they have read where the names of the characters are different to those that they are familiar with? Talk about the reference to 'Mama Margarita' and compare this to the use of Mrs and Madame in other countries. Do the children know of any other titles used to address people in other countries?

◆ Discuss the title 'Llamito'. What do the children think the story is about? Talk about the pronunciation of this word. What language does it come from? Have the children come across any other words that are spelled or pronounced like this?

Geography activities

◆ Look at an atlas with the children and talk about the location of South America and its countries, including Peru. Look at this continent in relation to other continents and in particular, Europe. In which direction would they have to travel to get to Peru? How might they travel? Which places would they cross to get there? Look at the other countries in the same latitude as Peru. Give the children blank maps of South America and ask them to label them with the main countries and cities.

◆ Set the children a research task to find out ten (or an appropriate number) facts about Peru or the continent of South America. Suggest some reference books, materials or websites to the class and give some headings, which might include the Andes mountains, animals, traditional food, named cities, weather, ancient civilisations. Ask them to report back in an appropriate timescale by making a wall display or giving a short talk to the rest of the class (which will also encourage speaking and listening skills).

◆ Get the children to use the Internet or a daily newspaper to record the weather temperatures for a main city in South America for a week. Ask them to write a brief weather report. It will be helpful for them to think about the type of vocabulary and phrasing that weather forecasters use. Phrases such as *overnight, temperatures plummet, cold spells, gathering storms*. Ask the children to listen to a forecast on the television and to list the phrases used to help them.

◆ Ask the children to think carefully about how the village in the text might look, and to draw a labelled picture to show the environment and the people in it. Then show them some pictures of Peru and ask them to compare how close their picture is to the real Peru.

◆ Discuss with the children the differences between pets and working animals. What do we have in our country? Can a pet also be a working animal? (Sheepdogs.) What other working animals can they think of around the world? (Camels, elephants, huskies, farm cats.) How are they used? What are the positives and negatives of working animals? (They are easier to use than machinery, cheaper to keep, often better adapted to the local conditions, for example camels or huskies. However, they also need space to be kept in, be properly looked after, and people may neglect them or treat them badly.)

Further literacy ideas

◆ Tell the children to use the information in the text to help them draw a family tree. Suggest they start with Maria Luisa and put in her family. A follow-up activity to this could involve the children writing out their own, or a friend's, family tree.

◆ Ask the children to underline or highlight those words which are adjectives, such as *craggy, dry, large*. Ask the children to check the meaning of these words in a dictionary and then to suggest one or more alternatives for each adjective used.

◆ The text refers to the fact that families in Peru are very united and look after one another. Ask the children to write a story entitled 'My family' about living with their family, or an incident when they have looked after a member of their family or a close friend. Make sure the children complete a story planner before starting their story so that they know what is going to happen at the beginning, in the middle and at the end.

◆ Using non-fiction reference books, ask the children to find out more about Llamas. This information could be presented to the class orally, or in the form of an illustration with accompanying information, including the source of the information which the children have used.

◆ The children could write a story with the title 'The Special Supper' about the supper that the family have to celebrate the birth of Ernestina's baby. Remind the children to include some of the characters in the text and to make reference to the setting of the extract.

◆ Discuss the use of capital letters in the extract for the names of people and places. Ask the children for other examples of capital letters being used other than at the start of a sentence.

◆ In a guided writing session, model how to summarise a story in the style of a book blurb. Use a different text initially for this modelling exercise and then ask the children to try and summarise 'Llamito' in the same way. They could start this exercise by writing bullet-pointed notes on individual white boards as the teacher reads the text.

Gregory Cool

Genre
story from
another
culture

"Come, I'll show you the river," said Lennox.

The air was shimmering hot. Gregory sat down in the shade. "I'd rather stay here," he said. "It's cool."

"Well, I go feed the goats, then dip in the river," said Lennox, and off he ran.

Gregory watched him go. Didn't want to play with him anyway, he thought. How can he move so fast in this heat?

He stretched out flat, and dreamed of hamburgers. But supper that evening turned out to be meat so hot and spicy, he could only eat the rice on his plate.

© Caroline Binch

Gregory Cool

Geography learning objectives
◆ To collect, record and analyse evidence (1b, 1c).
◆ To use fieldwork sketching techniques (2b).
◆ To use atlases and globes, and secondary sources of information (2c, 2d).
◆ To identify, locate and describe places (3a, 3b).
◆ To recognise how places fit within a wider geographical context (3g).
◆ Looking at a locality in a less economically developed country (6b).

Background notes
This is a story about a boy who goes to visit his cousin and family in the Caribbean, but the twist in the tale is that he finds he has a totally different outlook on life compared to his relatives, having been brought up in the UK.

Vocabulary
Shimmering, goats, hamburgers, evening, spicy, tropical forest, bananas.

Discussing the text
◆ Read the text, asking various children to take on the roles of Gregory and Lennox. Talk about the way these two characters might speak. Would they have different accents? Do the children have any suggestions as to what part of the world these two characters might come from? Ask them to give reasons for their answers.
◆ Talk about accents in general and how they indicate the place that a person originates from. Discuss whether or not it is possible to convey a person's accent when writing a story. Do the children know of any other stories where characters had an obvious accent – how was this conveyed?
◆ Ask the children what this text tells them about the characters in the story. What relation do the children think Gregory and Lennox are to one another? Is there any indication as to the age of the various characters? Which one do the children think is the oldest? Ask them to qualify their ideas. Ask them also to look at the way the thoughts are expressed – does Gregory feel a bit superior?
◆ Talk about the setting for the extract with the children. What information is given in the text about the environment? Ask the class to suggest a list of words that tell the reader about the setting (such as *The air was shimmering hot*). Ask them to share their ideas about the extract setting to the actual setting in the illustration. Do the children think they match? Considering the text and the illustration together, ask the children to suggest where the story is set.
◆ Talk to the children about illustrations in general. Are they necessary? Do the children think that the illustrations add to the atmosphere created by the text? How? (Draw their attention, for instance, to the types of trees in the picture.)

Geography activities
◆ Discuss with the children the type of location the story is set in. What are the characteristics of the place? What can the children surmise about the weather in this type of place? (Hot tropical forest in the Caribbean.)

◆ Ask the children to find the Caribbean Islands on a map. What are the names of the islands and towns in the Caribbean? Ask them to write down anything they know about the Caribbean (they may know about the sort of music played there, for example, such as steel bands).

◆ How does the environment differ where they live to that in the text? Ask them to draw sketches of the place where Gregory is visiting and their own area, showing settlements, types of vegetation and other features. Ask them to label the similarities and the differences

◆ Ask the children to plot a graph of weather information about the Caribbean, using information from the Internet or a newspaper, and to write a paragraph about summarising the main features. How does it differ from the weather where they live?

◆ Explain that in the Caribbean people often experience severe weather conditions, such as tropical storms, hurricanes and waterspouts offshore. Ask the children to research information about these extreme types of weather. The Met Office weather site will be helpful (www.met-office.gov.uk), as it gives good explanations and examples of such weather conditions. Make a class display entitled 'Extreme weather conditions'.

◆ Why do the children think people might be attracted to the Caribbean for a holiday? Give out some travel brochures and ask the children to find information about going to the Caribbean and to plan a holiday for their family. They will need to think about travelling there, costs of the holiday, any surcharges and the sort of clothes they will need to pack according to what sort of activities they will do whilst they are there.

Further literacy ideas

◆ Get the children to design a typical postcard to send from the Caribbean, and write in the message and the address correctly.

◆ Revise the use of speech marks with the children. Ask them to highlight the words that are spoken in the text. Tell them to make a note of the use of speech marks, and how each part of spoken text starts with a capital letter. Then give the children a different piece of text and ask them to put in the speech marks correctly.

◆ *He stretched out flat, and dreamed of…* Using this as a story starter, ask the children to imagine themselves in the setting described in the extract. They should focus on what elements of their current lives they would miss. Encourage them to think laterally about food, their homes, family and friends, and to make a list of things they would miss before they start as a planning aid.

◆ In the text the air is described as *shimmering hot*. Give the children a list of nouns, such as *wind* and *rain*, and ask them to come up with suggestions for adjectives that would describe the nouns.

◆ Ask the children to write a prequel to the story in the text. Prompt ideas by asking, *Why are the two boys in this place? How are they related? What have they been doing?*

◆ Tell the children you want them to imagine they are Gregory and to write a piece from his point of view. Encourage them to develop a character profile for Gregory. How does he feel about Lennox? What are his likes and dislikes? How does he feel about being in a strange environment?

◆ The author uses the verb *said* after the characters have spoken. Ask the children to find two different verbs each time it is used, such as *shouted*, or *whispered*. Remind the children that the words chosen must be suitable for what is being said and how it is being said.

◆ Make a class syllable chart using words from the text. Draw columns on a flip chart and fill in examples of words with one syllable, such as *hot*, two syllables, such as *supper*. Can the children find examples of three- or four-syllable words? (There are no four-syllable words in the extract, so ask the children to look in their own reading books.) Challenge the children to find as many syllables as possible in one word.

The house on stilts

Genre
*story in an
unfamiliar
setting*

The rain hammered relentlessly on the corrugated iron roof, splashing down into the gutters and overflowing into the air, droplets somersaulting their way to earth. The heavy, leaden skies promised more rain. Inside the house on stilts at the edge of the village, a grandmother, mother and daughter gazed anxiously at each other. From time to time each moved in turn to the window to stare out at the dripping tropical forest which surrounded the houses in the village.

It was over three hours since Bye, the toddler in the family, had disappeared. Only two years old, he had apparently wandered off on his own into the thick green jungle, which almost came up to the palisades surrounding the village. The sounds of dripping water were softened by the dense pattern of lianas and large-leaved plants, which covered the floor of the forest. Men from all the families in the village had been tracking and re-tracking across this part of the jungle, slashing their way through the undergrowth. Now it was rapidly growing too dark to see anything.

The flares from the torches marked the path of the men as they walked back to the village in the deepening darkness that was fast falling around them. They slowly walked past the house of sorrow and left the man to speak to his family.

"We'll try again at first light," he said softly. But the older woman shook her head sadly.

"He can't survive out there all night," she said. "There are just too many dangers." The mother and daughter were crying silently together.

At that moment, out of the darkness, came the sharp squealing from the pigs that lived under the stilted house. Grandmother tutted furiously under her breath and climbed down the ladder to investigate. She ducked under the house and began scolding the pigs. In the dark she could only just make out their shapes as they tore round and round a small bundle of grass in the middle of the floor. Suddenly the bundle moved and to her amazement Bye sat up yawning, rubbing his little fists into his eyes.

" Grandma!" he cried with joy. "I'm hungry!"

Paula Richardson

The house on stilts

Geography learning objectives

◆ To ask geographical questions (1a).

◆ To analyse evidence and draw conclusions (1c).

◆ To use secondary sources of information (2d).

◆ To recognise how people can improve or damage the environment (5a).

Vocabulary

Relentlessly, leaden, corrugated, gutters, somersaulting, tropical, palisades, lianas, survive, squealing.

Discussing the text

◆ Discuss the title of the story with the children. Where do they think that it might take place? Ask them: *What areas of the world might have houses on stilts? Why might they be built like this?* (They are built on stilts to allow the air to circulate and keep the inhabitants cool, and to deter animals from getting in.)

◆ Read the first paragraph of the story to the children. What do they understand by the word *anxious*? Why do the children think that the family were anxious? After reading this paragraph, discuss the setting for the story again. What clues can the children detect about the location now?

◆ Read the second paragraph of the story with the children and discuss the specialist vocabulary used, such as *palisades, lianas*. Do the children have any idea what these things are or might look like? Ask them to suggest the key words in the passage which indicate the nature of the environment.

◆ *He can't survive out there all night. There are just too many dangers.* Why do the children think that the grandmother said this? What dangers was she referring to?

◆ *The mother and daughter were crying silently together.* Discuss this phrase with the children. How could someone be crying silently?

◆ Discuss the meaning of any unfamiliar vocabulary in the text with the class, such as *relentlessly* or *leaden*.

Geography activities

◆ Discuss with the class where they think the story might be set. What are the clues they can find which will help them? (Torrential rain, house on stilts, tropical forest, lianas.) Can they name parts of the world which might have these features? (Mainly countries which lie in the tropical latitudes of the world.) Tell them the story is set in Thailand.

◆ Talk about what the village in the story might look like. Ask the children to draw the house and its surroundings, using only the story for guidance. Then ask them to look at pictures of such an environment in reference books and use the information they find to add or change features in their picture. Discuss with them how realistic the description was in the text. Could they draw the scene accurately from it? What extra information did they find for their pictures?

◆ Encourage the children to investigate the climate of such an area, for instance a tropical monsoon, by using information from a newspaper or the Internet. Ask them to graph their results and describe the pattern of weather that emerges. When did the temperatures reach their highest? Were there any dry months? When would it be best to visit the area?

◆ Discuss the lifestyle of the people in the village with the children. What sort of food would they have and where would it come from? (Grain, potatoes, yams, fruit; grown in the village or collected from the forest.) What might they get specifically from the forest? (Various fruits, but also small mammals and birds.) Why was the forest seen to be such a dangerous place in the story? What types of animals and birds might live there? Why would Europeans find it quite difficult to live in that area?

◆ Talk with the children about what life might be like for the people in the story? How would it differ from European life? What do they think will be the impact of European visitors on the life of the people there? Should tourists, for example, give medicines to the local people? (Any medicines would not be able to be sustained as a course, and would lower any natural immunity the local community has.)

Further literacy ideas

◆ Ask the children to identify alliteration in the text, such as *deepening darkness* and *fast falling*.

◆ Get the children to highlight the verbs used to describe the environment in the text, such as *hammered* and *somersaulted*. They could use a thesaurus to find similar and alternative words for those that they find.

◆ Ask the children to write a description of the emotions and feelings that the grandmother and mother might have experienced whilst waiting for news about the child. Then get them to write a contrasting piece about how they must have felt when the boy was found.

◆ The children could write a poem, using the descriptions of the environment in the text as a starting point, such as *heavy, laden skies* and *dripping tropical forest*.

◆ *Suddenly the bundle moved…* Get the children to use this as a starting point for an imaginative story.

◆ Ask the children to imagine that they are naturalists and to write a report describing and commenting on the environment described in the story. Encourage them to focus on the sights and sounds of the tropical forest.

◆ Examine the use of onomatopoeic words in the text, such as *slashing* and *scolding*.

◆ As a class, list the more difficult words in the text on a flip chart, such as *anxiously* and *investigate*. Look for strategies, for instance, mnemonics, which could help the children to learn how to spell them.

◆ Ask the children to write the story from the point of view of Bye, the toddler who went missing.

PHOTOCOPIABLE

Genre
brochure and
reference text

Peak National Park

Enjoying the Park

Walking is the number one outdoor activity in the National Park, with about 1600 miles (2575km) of public rights of way and 80 square miles (207 km²) of open access land on the northern and eastern moors. This gives an unparalleled choice for the walker, from gentle strolls through the limestone dales or on the converted railway trials, to some of the toughest walking in Britain across the peat bogs of the Dark Peak.

Climbers revel in the short but severe gritstone pitches provided on the 'edges' of the moors, like Stanage, Millstone and Froggatt, while longer, more technical climbing is found on the steep and sometimes overhanging crags of the limestone dales.

Traditional customs like the unique well-dressing ceremonies in many villages during the summer, attract many visitors. Others come to enjoy the wealth of historic buildings, like Peveril Castle at

© Peak-Pictures/Peak District National Park Authority

Castleton, Chatsworth and Haddon Hall near Bakewell, and Lyme Hall, near Stockport.

Details of all these attractions and other local events are contained in the National Park's annual newspaper *Peakland Post*.

© Peak-Pictures/Peak District National Park Authority

Caring for a Living Landscape

The Peak District National Park has adopted the phrase *Caring for a Living Landscape* as its vision statement. It reflects the fact that for many thousands of years, people have made their homes in the Peak District, creating the heritage of moors, farms, fields, woodlands and villages, which is shared with wildlife.

The National Park Authority works with others to keep the Peak a special place. It aims to keep the best and make changes for the better, with the aim of allowing future generations the opportunity to continue to be able to appreciate its beauty.

What is a National Park?

In Britain, a National Park is a large area of mostly privately owned land set aside for special protection because of its beautiful landscape. It is administered by a National Park Authority, whose job it is to keep the Park a special place for future generations. It does this by:

● conserving and enhancing the natural beauty, wildlife and cultural heritage, and
● promoting opportunities for the understanding and enjoyment of its special qualities.

In pursuing these aims, the Park Authority also has to foster the economic and social well-being of the people who live there.

which dominate in the centre and south of the district. This broad, rolling plateau at about 1000ft (304m) is split by river valleys into the dramatic, craggy dales so popular with visitors.

The Dark Peak, in contrast, is named after the clerical grey millstone grit rocks which underlie the moorland areas enclosing the limestone to the north, west and east like an upturned horseshoe. Fringed with steep 'edges' and weirdly weathered tors, this is the highest and wildest ground in the National Park, rising to 2088ft (636m) on the bleak tableland of Kinder Scout, north of Edale. In between these two distinct landscapes, the broad shale valleys of the Rivers Derwent and Wye are lined with trees. Here are found some of the largest settlements in the Park, like Bakewell, and the stately homes of Chatsworth and Haddon.

The Peak District National Park

The Peak District National Park covers 555 square miles (1438 km²) at the southern end of the Pennines between Sheffield and Manchester. It was the first to be set up in Britain in 1951 and although mostly in Derbyshire, covers parts of six counties. It is run by an independent local authority which includes representatives of the county and district councils and parish councillors and other members nominated by the Government.

About 38 000 people live in the Park. The major industries are farming and mineral extraction, although tourism is becoming increasingly important. Because of its accessibility and situation in the heart of England, the Peak District National Park is one of the most heavily visited National Parks in the world.

© Peak-Pictures/Peak District National Park Authority

Twin Peaks

In landscape terms, there are two Peak Districts, known as the Dark Peak and the White Peak. The White Peak takes its name from the underlying pale limestone rocks

Peak National Park

Geography learning objectives

◆ To use maps, atlases and photographs to identify, locate, and describe the Park (2c, 2d, 3a, 3b, 3c).

◆ To recognise change in the environment and reasons for it (4b, 5a).

◆ To recognise how and why people seek to manage environments (5b).

◆ To understand about issues arising from change in the environment (6d).

Vocabulary

National, protection, heritage, beauty, economic, Pennines, mineral extraction, tourism, accessibility, moorland, tors, plateau, dales, landscape, traditional, limestone.

Discussing the text

◆ Show the children the title of the first page of text, 'Peak National Park', on an OHP. Ask them to predict the type of text they will be looking at and what it might consist of. Make a list of their ideas on a flip chart, such as a map or a list of things to do. Then give the children both pages of text and ask them if there are any surprises. This particular leaflet contains quite a lot of text. Do the children think this is appropriate? Would they change it in any way? Discuss the possible audience for such a brochure. You may like to explain that, in addition to the text shown, there is a map with contact addresses on it in the original leaflet.

◆ Discuss the layout of the text including the size of the font, the typesize, the headings. Is the layout effective? Would the children change the layout in any way?

◆ Read through the text with the class. It may be appropriate to read the text over two or even three days. Highlight or make a list of vocabulary that is new to the children, such as *unparalleled* or *revel*. Discuss the meanings of some of the words with them. You may wish to use some of the vocabulary as the basis for a written dictionary exercise to be done later.

◆ Discuss the information given in the text. Have any of the children visited this area of the country? Do they recognise any of the descriptions or names of the places in the text?

◆ Discuss the 'vision statement' of the Peak National Park, *Caring for a Living Landscape*. What do the children think a vision statement is? Discuss this in relation to the school's 'mission statement'.

Geography activities

◆ Discuss with the children what is meant by a National Park. Use a map to show them where all the British National Parks are. What sort of locations do they have in common? (They are in higher areas of land, often not far from built-up places.) Ask the children to label a map of the British Isles to show the National Parks and their nearby towns. Which places do not have a National Park near them? (Scotland does not have any because there are many areas of wilderness which are not threatened by populated areas.) Discuss why it is necessary to have areas designated as National Parks? What might it stop people doing there? (It restricts development of the area.)

◆ Ask the children to write a definition of a National Park as if they were explaining it to someone who doesn't know what it is. Make sure they include why it is necessary to have them, what the characteristics of a Park area are, why people are drawn to them and what the Parks offer (remind the children that people do live and work in the Parks – they are not just open, deserted areas).

◆ Find the Peak National Park and other Parks on an atlas, or use a map website on the Internet (such as www.multimap.com) or an OS map to show the children in greater detail. Ask them a range of geographical questions, such as the location of, directions to and distances between different places, for example Castleton, Chatsworth or Bakewell.

◆ Ask the children to analyse what sort of view the brochure promotes about the Park. What messages does it convey? Why do they think this is done? Who is the brochure aimed at? (Tourists.) What sort of points would they include in a brochure of their locality? What would they not mention, and why?

◆ What problems do the children think that tourists bring to open areas such as this one? (Pathway erosion or litter.) Can these be solved? (Paths can be strengthened but any work will need to blend in with the environment. Similarly, litter bins and notices may be more intrusive than the litter itself.) Discuss how these problems and their solutions, or others, could be tackled.

◆ Ask the children to imagine they have been commissioned by the Peak National Park Authority to draw and illustrate a poster to encourage visitors to come to the area, but also to care for the area. Discuss what sort of things they will need to consider before making the poster.

◆ Using the information available, get the children to plan a stay in the area for a few days. What would they like to see and do? What sort of physical activities would be good? (There is a range to choose from: walking, climbing, sailing, orienteering, camping.) Suggest they plan the route from school, and include how they will get there and where will they stay.

◆ Ask the children to research areas in the Peak National Park which have interesting features or a history. These include Eyam (a plague village), Bakewell (famous for puddings and tarts), Peveril Castle, Chatsworth House, as well as the Blue John mines and other caverns. Well-dressing is a ceremony that takes place in the summer at wells and churches in the area.

Further literacy ideas

◆ The text makes reference to the *Peakland Post* newspaper. Discuss with the children the sort of articles that may appear in this publication. Using a writing frame ask the children to plan an appropriate article, for instance on the benefits of walking. These articles could be put together and a class newspaper produced.

◆ Ask the children to design adverts for the *Peakland Post*. They will need to think about the sorts of articles likely to be published in this type of newspaper and the likely readers, and target their adverts accordingly, such as for farm manure or walking boots.

◆ Give the children a section of the text and ask them to rewrite it in child-friendly style and language. This exercise may be better done as the follow-up to a shared writing lesson where you can model how to do this.

◆ Use a section of the text in a guided writing lesson to show the children how to make notes from a non-fiction text, by highlighting key words and then summarising the main points.

◆ Ask the children to write a narrative tale set in the Peak District. They can use information from the text to help them set the scene for the tale. Remind them to use descriptive vocabulary, and to plan the events of the story so that there is a beginning, middle and an end.

◆ In a shared writing lesson, ask the children to suggest improvements that could be made to the text. Draft a letter from the class or a group of children to the Peak National Park Authority, outlining these improvements.

◆ Ask the children to draft a list of questions that they would like to ask the authorities about the Park based on the information given in the text, for example how many visitors the park gets each year, and so on.

The Arctic

Genre
*non-fiction
text*

The Arctic

The Arctic is the area inside the Arctic Circle around the North Pole. It is a huge frozen ocean, surrounded by islands and by the northern coasts of Asia, Europe and North America.

The Arctic is cold all year round. In winter the sun never comes above the horizon, and the sea is frozen over. In summer, temperatures creep above freezing, the edge of the Arctic ocean melts, and for weeks the sun never sets. The Arctic Ocean is rich in plankton and fish. These are food for millions of sea birds, which nest in the Arctic in summer, and for seals, whales and other sea creatures.

Icebergs are created when the edge of the ocean melts in summer. Big parts of ice break off and float away, usually melting in warmer waters.

Ringed seal

These are the most commonly found seals in the Arctic region. They are also the smallest, weighing around 67kg and measuring no more than 1.5m in length. The seal's name comes from its markings – the spots and rings of marks on its skin. Its diet includes Arctic cod and shrimps. In summer the ringed seal moults and spends time out of the water – sunbathing!

Narwhal

The most interesting fact about this whale is the long tusk that the males have – only a small proportion of females develop a tusk. This tusk is actually a modified tooth, growing from the narwhal's jaw. Narwhals weigh around 1.5 tonnes and can be up to 5m in length. They live mainly offshore in the ice floes of the Arctic and feed upon small fish and squid.

The Arctic

Geography learning objectives

◆ To collect, record and analyse evidence (1b, 1c).

◆ To use atlases, globes and other secondary sources of information (2c, 2d).

◆ To use ICT to help in geographical investigations (2f).

◆ To locate, identify and describe what the Arctic is like (3a, 3b, 3c).

◆ To place the Arctic region in a wider world context (3g, 7b).

Vocabulary

Arctic Circle, icebergs, narwhal, ringed seal, arctic cod, plankton, mammal, sunbathing, North Pole, tusk.

Discussing the text

◆ Show the children the map on an OHP with the text covered up initially and ask them if any of them know anything about this part of the world. Do they know where it is in relation to the UK?

◆ Read the text entitled 'The Arctic' with the children; ask them which are the key words in the text – the ones that give them the main points of information. How would the children describe this text? (Informative, factual, or non-fiction.) What do they think are the characteristics of this type of text?

◆ Discuss the wildlife pictures with the children and ask if they are able to identify the creatures. What type of animals are they? (Mammals.) Discuss the pronunciation of the word *narwhal* with the children – why do they think it has this name. Does it come from the English language, or might it be from another one?

◆ Discuss with the class how often animals from the same family, such as the whale family, have similar names. Can the children think of other examples of animals or plants from the same family that have similar names (tits – blue tit, great tit)?

Geography activities

◆ Discuss with the children where the Arctic is located, using both an atlas and a globe. On the globe it should be possible to see that flying over the North Pole from Canada to Russia is a shorter route than flying from west to east (the Great Polar Route). Ask the children to try working out the shortest route from Canada to Russia, or from New York to Berlin. Would they go straight across the Atlantic, or is there a shorter way? Also, which do they think is the shortest route from London to Japan? (Remember to tell them to use a globe, not a map!)

◆ Discuss with the children why the routes in the above activity are the shortest to get from starting point to destination, but if they used a world map the 'apparent' shortest route is different. Can they tell you why this is? (Because we have to flatten the earth to make a map, so the shortest routes go off the top of the map and back onto it in another place.)

◆ Look at the countries that the Arctic Circle passes through around the world. Ask: *What does the Arctic Circle mark?* (Areas which will have almost complete daylight in summer and complete darkness in the winter.) Help the children to find Antarctica and the South Pole so they know the different locations of both places. Apart from being on opposite sides of the world how are these two places different? (The North Pole is frozen ice, but Antarctica is frozen land.)

◆ Show the children pictures of icebergs and floating ice-packs. Discuss how these would move and what noises they might make. Explain that often three quarters of an iceberg is underwater. How do they think this will affect any ships in the area?

◆ Read or tell the children the story of the Titanic. Talk about why the crew of the ship were taken unawares by the encounter with the iceberg – how had the iceberg reached so far south?

◆ Introduce the children to some of the animals which live in the cold climates of the Arctic and Antarctic zones. Encourage them to do some research to find out more about the wildlife in these places and to draw pictures of them. The narwhal is described as 5m in length. Measure this out on the floor to give a clear picture of how big the whale is. Ask the children how it compares to other animals in the Arctic, and then to other objects that they know of, such as a car. Make up a class display of the children's research into Arctic wildlife and get them to label their pictures with how each animal has adapted to life in cold conditions.

◆ What do the children think it would be like to live in almost total daylight in the summer and total darkness in winter? Ask them to look up what is meant by the phrases *midnight sun* and *Northern lights*. Then get them to write an account of living inside the Arctic Circle, and the experience of going to school, for example, in this environment.

◆ Read the children some stories about early expeditions to the Poles, such as those of Shackleton or Scott.

Further literacy ideas

◆ Ask the children to write a story set in the Arctic. They may need to use reference books to research information that will help them describe the setting. What sort of people, if any, live in this environment? Remind the children of the need to keep characters and plot realistic when basing their story on a factual place.

◆ Use the text as a starting point for investigating the use of dashes. Ask the children to find examples in their reading books, or other non-fiction reference books, of these being used. Make sure the children understand when these dashes should be used, and then present them with a selection of sentences, or a short passage, and ask them to put dashes in the correct places.

◆ Ask the children to choose either the narwhal or the ringed seal and to write a story from the animal's point of view in the first person. Remind the children to use the information given in the text in their stories, for example reference could be made to the narwhal's diet or size.

◆ Ask the children to write a piece of fiction about an iceberg being in the path of a boat they are on. Tell them to use appropriate language to make their description dramatic, as well as using information they have learned about icebergs to recreate them realistically in their story.

CHAPTER 2

Physical geography

Physical geography deals with the processes that shape the land, and the patterns and features which are associated with these processes.

While the study of places deservedly occupies a central position in primary geographical studies, physical geography is intimately connected to places in the way in which it influences the character of a place. It underlies any place study, as the weather and climate contribute to the character of a place.

Although there is only one specific physical geography theme in the National Curriculum at Key Stage 2 – water in the landscape – other aspects of physical geography can be picked up through place studies, including the local area of the school.

Included in this chapter are two items relating to earthquakes. They do not feature as part of the required programme of study at Key Stage 2, but they are of great interest to children and affect some of the places studied. Certainly, they will feature in the news on a number of occasions during a child's time in Key Stage 2.

Other selected texts in this chapter look at the weather or water themes in various ways, allowing flexibility of use according to how your school has organised its geography study units. In using these texts, look out for opportunities to develop children's knowledge and understanding of the *processes* involved in weather, climate and water in the landscape, the *patterns* (at different scales) which these processes produce, and the *features* which can be seen around us as a result.

Sinking sands

Genre
adventure story in a familiar setting

The mist was getting worse as they ran through the woods towards the sea. Karen was in the lead now, followed by Jane and then Peter. The path was muddy and they were only half-way round the course. Peter knew he was going to lose.

Then he had an idea. It was a risk, but Peter didn't care. He had to win.

They were running along the path beside the sea. The other runners were a long way behind, completely out of sight.

Soon Karen, Jane and Peter would turn away from the seashore. This was because the path had been swept away by the winter storms and the beach had a patch of dangerous sinking sand. There used to be a fence round this part of the beach, but it had been swept away by the sea.

The plan was very dangerous, but if it worked he was sure to come in first. No one would know. He would say he got in front of Karen and Jane in the big field near the quicksand. He would say that they couldn't have seen him running past them in the mist.

The mist was slowly turning to fog. No one could possibly see him cheating now. Peter could hardly make out the patch of quicksand in the fog but he knew the beach well – or thought he did.

He picked up speed, ran, jumped and with a gasp he almost made it. Almost.

Peter's feet hit soft mud. He heard a squelching, sucking sound. Suddenly he was up to his knees in the sand and still sinking.

Anthony Masters

Sinking sands

Geography learning objectives
◆ To ask geographical questions (1a).
◆ To communicate in various ways appropriate to the task and audience (1e).
◆ To use decision-making skills (2g).
◆ To identify water and its effects on the landscape and people, including the physical features of coasts (4a, 4b, 6c).

Background notes
This text tells part of the story of a cross-country race alongside the sea, and introduces the concept of quicksand. It takes place in mist and refers to the winter storms.

Vocabulary
Mist, sea, seashore, storms, sinking sand, quicksand, dangerous, fog, mud, coast.

Discussing the text
◆ *He had to win.* Why do the children think that Peter felt he had to win? Have they ever felt this way about anything?
◆ Talk about Peter's plan with the children. What did he plan to do? Why was it dangerous? What do the children think Jane and Karen would have thought about it if they knew? Would they have tried to stop him?
◆ *He knew the beach well – or thought he did.* Talk about this phrase with the children. Why was Peter so confident? How can we tell that maybe he was wrong from the text? (The use of the narrative voice after the dash.)
◆ Discuss with the children how the weather and the season affected events in the story. Do the children think the story would have been different in different weather conditions? What would have happened if it had been bright sunshine instead?
◆ Discuss paragraph five with the class. If Peter's plan had worked, what would have happened at the end of the race? What would Peter have said? How do the children think Karen and Jane would have reacted? Who do the class think would have been believed?
◆ Ask the children how Peter felt at the beginning of the text and how he felt at the end of the extract.
◆ Talk with the class about why Peter was proved wrong. Discuss how places can seem different in mist, fog and darkness. Was Peter also overly confident? Ask the children to find phrases in the text that tell them this, such as *It was a risk, but Peter didn't care.*

Geography activities
◆ Ask the children if they know what the landscape in the story is called (a coast). Discuss what a coast is (where the land meets the sea).
◆ As a class make a list of features of coasts. Start with the text, using examples such as *beach, sand, mud,* and then extend this list using the children's knowledge and a selection of pictures from the school's geography resources.

◆ Look at a map of the UK with the class to find the coastal areas and identify which of these areas have been visited by the children. Use this as a basis for a display, with labelled areas showing which have been visited.

◆ Using tourist brochures, or pictures of coasts and seaside towns, ask the children to label the physical features that can be found on them, such as the coast, waves, the tide, cliffs, a bay, beach, sand, shingle, sea.

◆ The children can use an Ordnance Survey map to find examples of sand and shingle beaches, making use of the key and symbols. Ask them to make a list of other symbols which relate to the sea.

◆ Explain to the children that sinking sands are also known as 'quicksands'. Do they think these only occur at the seaside? What other places could they get stuck in? (Marshes, bogs, or cut off by tide or rising floods.)

◆ Can the children think of other words for mist or similar phenomena? (Haze, smoke, smog.) What other weather can they think of that can reduce visibility? (Snow.) Where might this be dangerous? Get the children to select one type of visibility hazard and describe how and why it may be dangerous.

◆ Can the children explain how the sea has changed the coast in the text? How else might the sea change the coastline? (By eroding the beach, or by building up sand dunes.) When is this most likely to happen? (When the sea is at its most energetic during stormy weather.)

◆ As a class, collect pictures of sand and shingle beaches and locate them on wall maps. Extend this by collecting pictures of different beach and coast types (cliffs of rock or softer materials, steep beaches, rocky beaches, muddy beaches, tidal flats).

◆ Using the information in the text, ask the children to draw a cross-section sketch from the sea to the woods (showing sea, beach, quicksand, position of old fence, wood).

Further literacy ideas

◆ Ask the children to design a sign for the beach, warning of the dangers of the sinking sands.

◆ Get the children to make a list of all types of weather mentioned in the text. Ask them to extend this to list vocabulary for the different types of weather they can think of. What other words could be substituted to describe the weather in the text?

◆ Ask the children to list the adjectives that describe the weather and the environment in the story (such as mist, muddy path, fog, beach, quicksand).

◆ Ask the children to think about the setting for the story. They can use the text as a basis on which to write a description of the place.

◆ Ask the children to think about Peter, the main character. How would they describe him? Why do they think he acted as he did? After making a list of suggestions on a flip chart as a class, ask the children to write their own paragraph about Peter, describing his character.

◆ Ask the children to write an ending to 'Sinking sands'.

◆ The story is written in the third person. Identify with the class how the text tells us this (He picked up speed and so on). Ask the children to rewrite the story in the first person, giving them guidance first if necessary about how the verbs and pronouns will change, for example I picked up speed…

◆ Individually, get the children to write a letter to the local council about the dangers of the area described. Ask them to give their ideas about how to make the area safer.

◆ Explain to the class how the word dangerous has three syllables in it. Make a list on a flip chart of their suggestions for words in the text which have two or three syllables.

◆ Ask the children to find words in the text that have the long vowel pattern ou, such as round and course. What do they notice about the way these words are pronounced? Can they find other ways of pronouncing this letter combination?

Genre
information
text

From *The Magic Bus Inside the Earth*. Illustration © 1987, Bruce Degan. Text © Joanna Cole (Scholastic Inc).

From *The Magic Bus Inside the Earth*. Illustration © 1987, Bruce Degan. Text © Joanna Cole (Scholastic Inc).

SCHOLASTIC

Inside the earth

Geography learning objectives
◆ To ask geographical questions (1a).
◆ To collect and record evidence (1b).
◆ To use secondary sources of information (2d).
◆ To recognise some physical processes (4b).

Background notes
This text is based on the geology which lies beneath the surface and influences the shape of the land – soft rocks, hard rocks, sand, clay, and so on.

Vocabulary
Basalt, granite, igneous, lava, metamorphic, obsidian, pumice, quartzite, sedimentary, stalactite, stalagmite, marble, shale, slate, sandstone, limestone.

Discussing the text
◆ Ask the children if they know the names of any rocks. Record their answers on a flip chart and then show them the text entitled 'Rock collection'. Discuss the type of text it might be in terms of fiction and non-fiction.
◆ Discuss the format of the 'Rock collection' text with the children – the use of capitals, printing as opposed to joined-up writing, bold and underlining. Why do they think the text is presented in this way?
◆ As a class, discuss all the facts found in the 'Rock collection' text.
◆ Does it matter where they start reading the texts? Ask the children to consider whether parts of the texts could stand on their own or be taken away. Is this the same for a fiction text?
◆ Discuss where this type of text might be found, for example in a museum. Have the children seen examples of this type of text? Ask them to recall where.
◆ Discuss with the children how the different syllables of each word are separated in the 'Earth science words' text. Do the children know what the words in brackets are doing? Explain how these words are being spelled phonetically. Pronounce some of the words for the children and see if they can tell which country the text is from (it's American).
◆ Discuss the layout of the text on the blackboard. Why do the children think some letters are in upper case? (To show emphasis.)

Geography activities
◆ Use some examples of rocks to pass around among the children for them to feel. Ask them to explain what they are like. (Smooth, rough, jagged, coloured?) How do they think we get pieces of rock? Where do they come from?
◆ Choose some rocks containing minerals and get the children, working either individually or in pairs, to use a magnifying glass to look more closely at the rock and then describe it in detail. Can

other children recognise the rock sample from their descriptions?

◆ Develop a rock study by looking at fossils with the children, explaining that these are made from plants and creatures which have died and become encased in the materials which form the rock. Can they explain why we find many fossils in sedimentary rocks but not in the other types? (Get them to think about how the fossils get there in the first place.)

◆ Look around the school with the children and, using a large map to record their findings, get them to label where the different types of rock materials have been used (remember that clay is a rock, which is used to make bricks – this is actually a good example of metamorphism).

◆ Discuss other building materials with the class, such as bricks, glass and concrete. Where do they think these come from? Do they have a rock basis? (Yes, they are all made from rock – remember that sand is also a rock.)

◆ Build a class rockery or rock garden, and encourage the children to bring in their own samples. Label each rock, describing its type and identifying where it came from.

◆ Get the children to do some observational drawings of rocks and fossils, and to make a card describing what each one is and where it came from.

◆ Ask the children to identify what types of rock there are in their area. Every place has a rocky surface below the soil, even if the rock is unconsolidated, such as sand or clay. They could use a local map to look for references to rock types. Are there any clues in names, old industrial workings or features?

Further literacy ideas

◆ Allocate each child two rocks from the 'Rock collection' text and ask them to write a series of sentences from the notes given. Encourage them to use different paragraphs in their description of each rock.

◆ Get the children to sort the names of the rocks in both texts into alphabetical order. Discuss spelling strategies to help them to learn to spell some of the words.

◆ As a class get the children to say some of the rock words out loud and to clap out the syllables in each.

◆ Devise some questions which require the children to search for clues in the texts, for example *Indian arrowheads are made from* _____.

◆ Ask the children to search the texts for words which contain smaller words within them, such as pu*mice* or ba*salt*.

◆ Give the class another set of words within a theme, such as water words, and ask the children to write how they should be pronounced using the format in the 'Earth science words' text, for example tributary (trib–yew–tear–ey). Encourage them to use capital letters where they think the stress would fall.

◆ In pairs or small groups ask the children to prepare a similarly laid-out description as that in the 'Rock collection' text, drawing on animals or plants, listing, for example, *Name – snake, Type – reptile, Where found – moorland.* Ask them to add pictures to their descriptions and compile a class display in the same layout as the text.

◆ Investigate derived words in the texts, such as igneous (ignite) or sedimentary (sediment).

◆ Using the 'Rock collection' text introduce or revise work on possessive apostrophes, for example *Phil's rock.* Ask the children to write about their classmates, such as *Peter's hair is….*

◆ Get the children to use non-fiction books to find out more about the three types of rock – sedimentary, igneous and metamorphic. Ask the children, working in groups, to prepare a poster explaining each, or just one of, the three types.

Weather forecast

Forecast for today, 7 February

Rain and drizzle gradually clearing most parts from north-west; clearer weather following, with blustery showers, mainly in north-west.

© Digital Vision Ltd

The Midlands

Much of today cloudy with rain at times and the best chance of drier weather later this afternoon. Temperatures rising only slowly. Maximum temperature 9 deg C (48 deg F).

Northern Scotland

All parts will have sunny spells this afternoon but frequent showers coming into the west. Strong south-westerly winds. Maximum temperature 8 deg C (46 deg F).

Southern Scotland

Sunny spells this afternoon with frequent showers in the west. Mainly dry over Fife, Lothians and Borders. Quite windy. Maximum temperature 8 deg C (46 deg F).

Wales

A cloudy, mild day with any remaining rain clearing south-east this afternoon. Fresh to strong south-westerly winds. Maximum temperature 11 deg C (52 deg F).

South-east England

Cloudy with outbreaks of rain and turning misty later. A fresh to strong south-westerly wind. Maximum temperature 11 deg C (52 deg F).

Devon and Cornwall

Mainly cloudy with periods of drizzle but some drier interludes. Minimum temperature 7 deg C (45 deg F).

Northern Ireland

Most places will be drier by lunchtime with a few sunny intervals this afternoon and just scattered blustery showers. Maximum temperature 10 deg C (50 deg F).

Eastern counties

Cloudy with outbreaks of rain or drizzle and a fresh south-westerly breeze. Maximum temperature 11 deg C (52 deg F).

Yorkshire and Lincolnshire

Rain, locally heavy in Pennine districts at first will clear away during the afternoon with brighter breezier conditions soon following. Maximum temperature 10 deg C (50 deg F).

European temperatures (deg C/deg F)				
Alicante	17	63	Lanzarote	21	70
Amsterdam	9	48	Luxembourg	6	43
Ankara	3	37	Madrid	12	54
Athens	15	59	Mahon	15	59
Barcelona	15	59	Marseille	14	57
Belgrade	14	57	Milan	9	48
Bilbao	13	55	Moscow	3	37
Bordeaux	11	52	Naples	15	59
Brest	11	52	Nimes	15	59
Brussels	10	50	Oslo	-1	30
Bucharest	11	52	Paris	10	50
Budapest	7	45	Porto	16	61
Cagliari	14	57	Prague	7	45
Copenhagen	7	45	Rimini	13	55
Dublin	12	54	Rome	16	61
Dubrovnik	16	61	Seville	16	61
Faro	16	61	Stockholm	4	39
Frankfurt	8	46	St Petersburg	4	39
Geneva	8	46	Tel Aviv	22	72
Gibraltar	16	61	Venice	10	50
Helsinki	3	37	Vienna	3	37
Istanbul	12	54	Warsaw	10	50
Lagos	31	88	Zurich	5	41

Based on information supplied by the Met Office © Crown copyright.

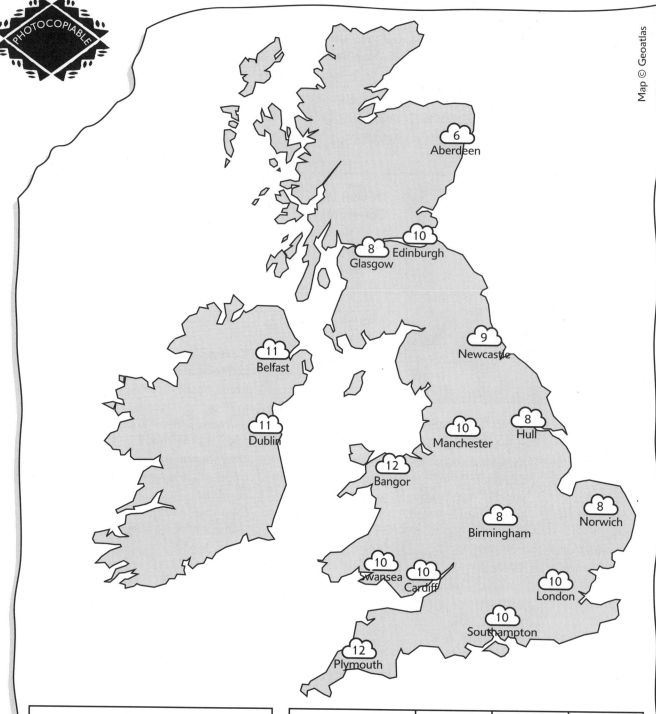

Map © Geoatlas

High tides

London B'ge	0701	5.9m	1943	5.7m
Dover	0415	5.6m	1657	5.3m
Liverpool	0437	7.3m	1719	7.3m
Hull	1158	7.0m	-	-
Penzance	1014	4.3m	2254	4.2m
Leith	0836	4.3m	2056	4.3m
Weymouth	1153	1.4m	-	-
Aberdeen	0718	3.3m	1941	3.4m
Belfast	0454	2.9m	1716	2.9m
Harwich	0509	3.3m	1753	3.2m

'Not to be used for navigation' © UK Hydrographic Office.

Air pollution	In rural areas	In towns and cities away from busier roads	In towns and cities next to busier roads
Northern Ireland	3 (Low)	3 (Low)	1 (Low)
London	-	3 (Low)	3 (Low)
Midlands	3 (Low)	3 (Low)	1 (Low)
North-east England	3 (Low)	3 (Low)	2 (Low)
North-west England	3 (Low)	3 (Low)	2 (Low)
South-east England	3 (Low)	3 (Low)	1 (Low)
South-west England	3 (Low)	3 (Low)	2 (Low)
East Anglia	3 (Low)	3 (Low)	1 (Low)
Wales	3 (Low)	3 (Low)	2 (Low)

Air pollution is on a scale of 1-10

Low (1-3)   Moderate (4-6)   High (7-9)   Very high (10)

Based on information supplied by the Met Office © Crown copyright

Weather forecast

Geography learning objectives

◆ To ask geographical questions (1a).

◆ To collect, record and interpret evidence (1b).

◆ To analyse evidence and draw conclusions (1c).

◆ To use a variety of sources of information (2d).

◆ To use a variety of means of communication, including ICT (1e, 2f).

◆ To recognise a variety of weather patterns (4b).

Vocabulary

Cloudy, rain, showers, misty, mild, drizzle, blustery, sunny spells, interludes, temperature, forecast, high tide, air quality.

Discussing the text

◆ Talk about the different ways in which the information is recorded in order to minimise the space used, for example in tabular form.

◆ Discuss the layout of the text, headings, typesize, and so on. Get the children to compare this layout with that of weather reports in other newspapers. What are the main differences and similarities?

◆ Discuss the use of abbreviations in the text, such as *deg C*. Ask the children to suggest what these abbreviations might mean.

◆ Ask the children different questions about the text, such as *What is the temperature in Cardiff?*

◆ Discuss possible audiences for the general weather forecast and the regional forecasts. How might the language differ for different audiences? (Get the children to think of how the language would have to be changed for younger readers.)

◆ Can the children think of the pros and cons of forecasting the weather? Who needs to know the weather forecast and why? What happens when the weather forecasters get it wrong, for example with the great storm of 1987?

Geography activities

◆ As a class, make a list of all the different types of information that are provided in the text (temperatures in Europe, regional forecasts) and record them on a flip chart. Then devise an oral quiz for the class, to develop knowledge about locations in the UK and all the different types of weather information available, asking questions such as *What will the weather be like in Devon?*

◆ Ask the children to look at the map of the UK and to write a brief account of the weather in their local area. They could do this on their own or in pairs.

◆ Choose five or six other locations and ask the children, working in pairs, to write the forecast for these areas. Remind them to use appropriate/accepted weather descriptions, such as *patchy light rain, widespread showers*.

◆ Ask the children to identify the warmest, coldest, driest and wettest places in Wales, Scotland, Northern Ireland, Republic of Ireland and England, and to highlight these on the map of the UK.

◆ Look at the other information displayed – the high tides and the air quality. Who do the children think would be interested in these pieces of information? (Anyone going out to sea; or environmentalists or those suffering from asthma, respectively, for example.) Discuss what sort of weather conditions might lead to poor air quality. (Settled weather, which could be either bright and clear or foggy, but with little wind.) Ask the children to find the places mentioned in the tide tables on a map, and to then plot the way the tide flows around the UK by noting the times of the high tides.

◆ The text provides an opportunity to locate regions in the UK, for example South-east England, the Midlands, and so on. Get the children to locate them in an atlas or a map of the UK, and then to mark them on a class wall map.

◆ Temperatures are given for a number of UK and European cities. Get the children to 'adopt' a city, and to look up and graph the temperature there for a specific length of time (a week, month or longer). They could use an Internet weather site or a daily newspaper to find the information.

◆ The previous activity can be followed up by getting the children to use resources such as the Internet and library books to develop a fact file on their adopted city and/or country. These can be presented and displayed in the classroom at a suitable time.

Further literacy ideas

◆ Select a portion of the text for the children and ask them to put the information into full sentences, using capital letters, full stops and appropriate punctuation. They might also embellish the text to make it more interesting to the reader, drawing upon their knowledge of how to use adjectives and adverbs within sentences.

◆ Record a weather forecast from the TV or radio and play it to the class. Ask the children to record the main information given and to reduce this information to note form.

◆ Ask the children to make up a list of comprehension questions for a partner about the text. Then, working in pairs, get them to swap their questions with their partner and work through each other's comprehension questions.

◆ Ask the children to use highlighter pens to mark the key facts and figures on the text.

◆ Ask the children to use the information in the text to help them write a script for a TV weather forecast in groups. Tell them they should concentrate on including only appropriate information (such as that highlighted in the previous activity) and keeping the summary concise. They could then perform their forecast to the rest of the class – and have it recorded on video if possible.

◆ Ask the children to identify the descriptive words in the text and place them into categories, for example adverbs (*mainly*) and adjectives (*cloudy*).

◆ As a class exercise, investigate comparative and superlative adjectives in the text, for example *wet: wetter, wettest*.

◆ Provide the children with a cloze procedure exercise, where they have to find answers from the text, for example *Blustery showers will be mainly in the* _____.

CHECKS BY THE SEA

- Always swim close to the beach and in line with the shore.
- Never climb on cliffs – keep away from the edges – even gentle slopes can be dangerous when wet.
- Never dive or jump from piers, groynes or breakwaters etc., and take care when entering the sea

Don't swim
- near pipes (outflows), rocks, breakwaters and piers
- when the red flag is flying
- if you feel unwell, or tired
- for at least an hour after a meal
- when you are cold or very hot
- if you have been drinking alcohol
- where powered boats are operating
- where surf boards or sailcraft are active.

Don't stay in the water too long
- you may become cold and tired.

IN THE SUN

The Sun's rays can cause skin cancers

To protect yourself from the sun remember

Slip – on a long sleeve 'T' shirt

Slap – on a broad brimmed hat

Slop – on some sun cream

Take Care
- Children need to be supervised by an adult at all times, especially near the sea. Toddlers can be knocked over by waves and can quickly drown – even in shallow water.
- Make sure you always know where everyone from your group is – if anyone goes swimming or leaves the beach.
- Beware of being trapped by the incoming tide, or the sea circling behind you. Find out about the tide times from tide tables and from the Coastguard, Lifeguards or notice boards on the beach. Always keep an eye on water levels.
- Avoid rip tides and strong currents beneath the surface. Calmer water between areas of surf usually indicates a dangerous rip current which may carry you out to sea.
- Watch out for large waves and the wash from passing vessels. They can sweep you off your feet even if you think you are standing somewhere safe.

© RNLI

Checks by the sea

Geography learning objectives

◆ Use secondary sources to find out information (2d).

◆ Make comparisons between places and through time (3f).

◆ To understand some of the dangers at the seaside (3d, 4b, 6c).

◆ To recognise coastal features, both physical and human (4a, 6c).

Background notes

Seaside holidays are very popular, even if many families take them in another country, rather than in the UK. This text uses a safety poster as a starting point to investigate concepts about the seaside and its features.

Vocabulary

Calm, dangerous, Coastguard, Lifeguard, edge, shallow, beach, rocks, groynes, piers, remote, cliffs, slopes, waves, snorkel.

Discussing the text

◆ Who do the children think the poster is written for and where might it be displayed? Have they come across posters like this one? If so, where did they see them and did they carry the same information?

◆ Discuss the layout of the text with the class, drawing attention to the main features – the bullet points and sub-headings. Discuss why some parts of the text are in bold type.

◆ Talk about the content of the information on the poster. Why do the children think the writer chose this information? Has anything been left out? If so, why do they think this happened? (Talk about the need for conciseness to make a poster powerful.)

◆ Do the children think the tone of the text is formal or informal? Why do they think it is written in this way?

◆ Explore the tense of the text. Can the children explain why it is in the present tense?

◆ Discuss the difference between fact and opinion, and ask the class to decide which information on the poster is factual.

◆ Ask the children to think about the colours which might be used to print this poster in order to attract the reader.

Geography activities

◆ Record on a flip chart the children's suggestions for words in the text which identify the place as a coastal area (such as rocks, shallow, waves, tides, breakwaters, cliffs). Discuss with the children where these would be in relation to the coast. (It may be helpful to look at some pictures of different coastlines.) Then ask them to draw a large picture of a coastal area and include all of their identified features and to label them. Then ask them to label their drawing with some of the dangers identified on the poster.

◆ Ask who in the class has been to the seaside! What did they do there? What was it like? Discuss with the class the sort of features which would be found at the seaside and ask them to put the list into two categories – natural and human features.

◆ Provide the class with a map of the UK and a list of seaside towns. Ask them to mark these onto the map and label them, using atlases to help. Ask where the nearest seaside place to school is and which route they could take to get there. Ask them to identify the roads they would use and towns they would pass or bypass. Working in pairs, get the children to write instructions on how to get to a seaside destination of their choice from school.

◆ Do the children think that seaside towns are similar to or different from those in Victorian times? Get them to explain how and why they are different. What is still the same? Make a two-column list on a flip chart, with headings 'The same' and 'Different', and ask the class to list all the things which would have been the same or different in Victorian times as today.

◆ Collect a series of pictures of seaside places, including those overseas. (Postcards and travel brochures will be good sources for these.) Ask the children to identify as many features as they can on the pictures. Can they draw a simple sketch of one of them and label the features?

◆ What sorts of jobs do the children think would be available at seaside resorts in the summertime? What happens to a resort in the winter? (Use pointers such as *What attracts tourists to the seaside? How important is the weather?*) Organise a 'homework survey', where the children ask someone at home what attracts them to the seaside. They could prepare questions, such as *What do you like about the seaside? What do you not like?* Finally, ask them to make a graph of their information so that comparisons can be drawn between the responses all the children have gathered.

Further literacy ideas

◆ Ask the children to write a similarly styled information leaflet for another potential danger area, for example walking by a busy road.

◆ The children can highlight the key words in the text and use these to make up a poster of warnings for very young children.

◆ Some of the sentences lack detail, for example *Always swim close to the beach* or *Never climb on cliffs*. Ask the children to expand some of these sentences outlining reasons for the instruction.

◆ Focus on *Don't* to investigate contractions. Ask the children to list other contractions that they know, and to write out the full version next to each one.

◆ *Beware of being trapped by the incoming tide.* Get the children to use this as an opening sentence for a story.

◆ Explain to the children that the poster is produced by the RNLI. Ask them to find out what these letters stand for. Use this as a basis for the children to discover other acronyms, such as BBC.

◆ Ask the children to find coast-related words in the text such as *breakwaters, piers, groynes*. They can use dictionaries to find the meaning of words they don't understand and make a class 'Coastal word book'.

Genre
information/
instructions
in the form of
a list

Preparing for an **earthquake**

This list is to help you get ready. Be sure to read it and then pin it up somewhere so you can find it if needed. Has everyone in the family read it?

■ Have torches ready – also a portable radio and extra batteries.

■ Have the first aid kit and the fire extinguisher handy.

■ Store a few litres of water per family member.

■ Have one week's food stored preferably outside the house if possible.

■ Strap down the boiler.

■ Do not place beds under windows or big mirrors.

■ Listen to announcements on the radio.

■ Have a plan to reunite the family day or night up to 50 miles away.

Preparing for an earthquake

Geography learning objectives

◆ To be able to use secondary sources to find information (2d).

◆ To learn about emergency procedures in school and their own homes (2g).

◆ To understand how an earthquake can affect daily lives (4b).

Background notes

Although earthquakes are most common along the main earthquake belts of the world, they can occur anywhere. In the UK, we usually experience very minor ones. This text can be used as a starting point for investigating the effects of earthquakes and being prepared for other, more common emergencies.

Vocabulary

Earthquake, torch, portable, boiler, announcement, tremor, damage, structure, collapse, foundation, destruction.

Discussing the text

◆ Place the text on an OHP and show the class the title *Preparing for an earthquake* and explain that the text is a list of instructions Can the children predict what instructions might be on the list?

◆ Give out the text to the children and discuss any unfamiliar vocabulary in the text, such as *preferably*.

◆ Discuss the text with the class in the context of its being a public information document. Discuss the fact that the language is often impersonal and how this is different from other kinds of text. Do the children know of any other such documents?

◆ Discuss with the children where the text might be found (in a public library, or in a private house).

◆ Talk with the children about the reasons why some of the instructions are given, for example why should beds not be put under windows or big mirrors?

Geography activities

◆ Discuss the implications of each of the items on the list with the children. Explain that the need to have everything in place and the known location of each item is important, as an earthquake can happen suddenly and without warning. They also need to understand the need for torches and battery-powered radios as power supplies will be the first service to be disrupted.

◆ Do the children think such a list would be needed in Britain? What situation might it be more likely that we would need a similar list for? (Flooding or a cut in power supplies.) Ask if anyone has had a power-cut in their home. What was it like? How did they manage in such a situation? Do they have emergency supplies at home, and if so, what are these and where are they kept? Get the children to work in pairs or small groups to prepare a list of items they would want to have in an 'emergency pack' which they could take at a moment's notice if there was an emergency situation (they could include items not on the list, such as a favourite teddy or a hand-held computer game).

◆ What do the children think would be the different effects of a major earthquake on a large city and in open countryside? Get them to write a paragraph describing the effects of an earthquake of some magnitude in both a town and in a village out in the countryside.

◆ Explain that a plan for reuniting the family is very important after an emergency situation. Do the children know why this is? Why is it recommended to think about the meeting place being up to 50 miles away. Make a list of reasons as a class. In groups, the children can make a list for their own house with the appropriate advice for an emergency. Get them to think about where they would store items such as torches, where they would keep emergency telephone numbers and what these should be. If there isn't a telephone in the house where would calls be made from?

◆ Look at a telephone book and a Yellow Pages directory with the children. Give a list of mishaps which might occur (roof tiles blown off, a tree fallen down in the garden, burst pipes) and for each of these ask groups of children to look up suitable people or services to contact.

◆ Ask the children to imagine their house was without electricity for a week. Get them to list all the things which would not work throughout the day. Ask them to also list suggestions for things they could use instead. What would be the most difficult thing to be without?

◆ What emergency materials and procedures are in place in school? (Fire drills, rules and extinguishers, parking rules, first aid kits.) What happens if it snows very hard and the school is closed? How do the children think that people gain this information? (Local radio, notices outside school.) If the children do not know the answers to these questions, organise an investigation activity so that they are aware of them.

Further literacy ideas

◆ Ask the children to find out more about the effects of an earthquake. Make sure they start by making a list of what questions they want to find answers to, and then to research the information from appropriate reference sources.

◆ Tell the children to imagine they are going to interview the survivor of an earthquake. They should write a list of questions and predict the answers.

◆ Ask the children to write a story called 'Trapped' involving an individual or group of people who are trapped in the aftermath of an earthquake – encourage the children to bring a sense of fear and immediacy into their writing by composing the story in the first person.

◆ Ask the children to write a diary entry for someone trapped in an earthquake, waiting to be rescued.

Quake shocks Seattle

6.8-magnitude temblor "hits you in the stomach"

by Patrick McMahon

Seattle – This business capital of the Pacific Northwest has been preparing for a big earthquake for more than 10 years. But when it finally struck Wednesday, it still jolted the city's psyche.

A midmorning 6.8-magnitude earthquake made skyscrapers sway, damaged overpasses, knocked out power, jammed cell phones and injured more than 250 people. One woman died of a heart attack.

"At first, it was 10 seconds and it's laid back. We've had these before. Have another latte," said Jean Tarbox of Seattle, who was near the University of Washington campus. "Suddenly, it hits you in the stomach, and you find yourself holding on to the doorway."

Thousands of airline passengers were delayed when the control tower at Seattle-Tacoma International Airport was damaged.

Damage from the quake – felt from Canada to Portland, Ore. – might exceed $1 billion, said Washington Gov. Gary Locke, who declared a state of emergency.

But it wasn't worse because of a geological stroke of luck: The quake began 30 miles underground.

"That means everybody had at least 30 miles of rock between them and the place the shaking was produced, so it had time to die down," said Lucy Jones, chief seismologist in the US Geological Survey's office in Pasadena, Calif.

By contrast, a quake of similar magnitude that basted Northridge, Calif., in 1994 began 12 miles underground. The result: 72 dead, 9,000 injured and $25 billion in damage.

Wednesday's quake was the region's worst since a 7.1-magnitude temblor with three times the strength in 1949 killed eight near Olympia. Maybe it wasn't the Big One, Seattle mayor Paul Schell said, "but this is as close as we want to get."

Office workers in downtown Seattle and Portland, Ore., fled buildings when the temblor struck at 10.55 am. It was centred 35 miles southwest of Seattle.

Officials credited earthquake preparedness programs for limiting damage. Millions of dollars have been spent strengthening buildings.

"There's been a really major effort," Jones said. She said Seattle and its business leaders have "made huge strides in the last 10 years" improving building codes.

The quake damaged many building from Seattle south to Olympia, the state capital. The Capitol dome developed a visible crack.

Bricks fell from the top of Starbucks headquarters in south Seattle. About 30 people were briefly trapped atop a swaying Space Needle, a Seattle landmark.

Screams and falling overhead lights even forced Seattle's most prominent citizen, Microsoft founder Bill Gates, to cut short a speech at a technology conference downtown.

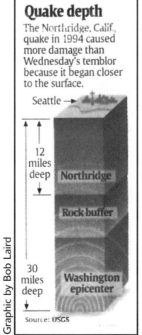

Quake depth

The Northridge, Calif., quake in 1994 caused more damage than Wednesday's temblor because it began closer to the surface.

Seattle →

12 miles deep

Northridge

Rock buffer

30 miles deep

Washington epicenter

Source: USGS

Graphic by Bob Laird

Quake shocks Seattle

Geography learning objectives

◆ To analyse evidence and draw conclusions (1c).
◆ To use appropriate geographical vocabulary (2a).
◆ To use secondary sources of information (2d).
◆ To identify how and why places change (3e).
◆ To recognise the impact of physical processes (4b).

Background notes

This newspaper report of an actual earthquake, on 28 February 2001, can be used to develop the preceding extract, 'Preparing for an earthquake', looking at the effects experienced by people as well as following through the geographical references.

Vocabulary

Quake, Seattle, magnitude, Pacific, skyscraper, overpass, campus, control tower, international, $, billion, emergency, geological, seismologist, technology, downtown.

Discussing the text

◆ Discuss the layout of the article with the children, focusing on the heading, sub-heading and the use of different fonts. How does this affect the reader? Compare the text with other newspaper articles which use different fonts, for example a UK broadsheet or tabloid. Which do the children find easiest to read, and why?

◆ Ask the children to look at the headline and predict the story in the article. Ask them to consider and suggest alternative headings once they've understood what the content of the article is about.

◆ Discuss with the class how the diagram helps the reader to understand how the earthquake affected the surrounding area.

◆ Talk about what the children already know about earthquakes. On a flip chart make a list of questions which the children would like to ask to find out more about them, and discuss where they might go to find answers, such as encyclopedias, CD-ROMs, books on earthquakes and volcanoes.

◆ Discuss the style of the newspaper report. Draw the children's attention to the fact that the writing is immediate and uses a lot of standard phrases and shorthand – especially in the headlines and sub-headings. Is this the only style that newspaper journalism, or other journalism, adopts? (Compare broadsheet, tabloid and magazine styles, for example.)

◆ Pick out the word *centered* in paragraph ten and ask the children what they notice about it (the spelling!). Ask them what this suggests to them (that it is an American source). Go through the text with the children and identify spellings, words and phrases which suggest that this extract is from an American paper, rather than a UK one.

Geography activities

◆ Discuss with the children what an earthquake is and how it differs geographically from a volcanic eruption.

◆ Ask the children what the short-term effects of a major earthquake are. What needs to be done in the few days following the event? In America, for example, the declaration of a state of emergency will trigger State funds and aid packages. What do they think the more long-term needs would be? This will involve the class considering financial aid and support of various kinds, such as help in rebuilding homes, repairing roads and bridges, caring for the injured and perhaps support for relatives of any dead (only one person in this case – but things might have been different in the rush hour). What about an earthquake or major disaster in a poorer country of the world? Aspects to consider in this instance will be the poor quality of the building materials often used to erect high-rise housing blocks, which often lack anti-earthquake design. Following this discussion, ask the children to write a short piece entitled 'Help after the earthquake', in which they explain what help would be needed under three headings – 'Immediate needs', 'Short-term help' and 'Longer-term support'.

◆ Look at where earthquakes occur with the children Study a large world map and discuss the links between the countries and the plate boundaries/lines of weakness. Find out where the vulnerable countries are and record these on a flip chart. Are there any major cities on the boundary line? (Los Angeles is a prime example. Many people commute into work from over 50 miles away so that their family homes are in a safer location.)

◆ Ask the children to consider whether earthquakes ever occur in Britain. Have they felt an earthquake or tremor? It is estimated that up to 20 small quakes occur in the UK every year, mainly in the Scottish Highlands, but little effect is usually felt above ground. Just occasionally bigger shockwaves are recorded, such as in Wrexham (1990), Lleyn Peninsula (1984), Home Counties (1938). Children can use a reference book to look up interesting earthquakes which have occurred in the UK as well as elsewhere in the world.

◆ Ask the children to imagine that an earthquake has occurred in their local area. Ask them to discuss in groups how the area might be affected. Get them to look up the scales for measuring the magnitude and severity of an earthquake, such as the Richter Scale or the Mercalli Scale. They should consider what might happen to buildings and other features of their environment with a quake measuring, for example 4 in strength on the Richter scale.

Further literacy ideas

◆ Get the children to highlight in different colours on the text the various verb tenses used, making a key to express what tense each colour represents. Then ask them to change passive sentences to active, and vice versa.

◆ Suggest the children use dictionaries to find the meaning of unfamiliar words, such as *psyche*, *geological*.

◆ Ask the children to write a short piece entitled 'A quiet cup of coffee', or something similar, from the point of view of someone caught inside a café during the earthquake.

◆ The text states that this earthquake was the worst in the area since 1949. Ask the children to write a newspaper report in a similar style describing that event.

◆ Ask the children to find examples of emotive words or phrases used in the text, such as *Suddenly, it hits you in the stomach…* Can they change the impact of the article by changing these words and phrases?

◆ The text contains a number of comments from individuals caught in the earthquake. Ask the children to devise a series of interview questions to ask these, or other locals. Include Bill Gates – (do the children know who he is?). Then, in pairs, get them to swap interview questions and write possible answers to each other's questions.

Anna, Grandpa and the big storm

Genre
story in a familiar setting

Anna's fingers were numb with cold. She could hardly hold on to the railing of the engine. Often she had seen the horses racing down the street to a fire. Now they plodded along very, very slowly through the deep snow.

No one spoke. The wind roared and shrieked. The snow blinded them. One fireman jumped off the engine and tried to lead the horses forward.

Anna huddled against the side of the engine, hiding her face in her arms. It was taking them such a long time to reach the fire station.

Just then, the horses turned abruptly to the left. The next moment they were inside the stable, snorting and stamping their hooves.

Several men ran forward to unhitch the engine. Everyone began brushing the icy snow off their clothes.

Suddenly Grandpa became very serious. "The thermometer says five degrees above zero, and the temperature is still dropping. We must get home as fast as possible. Mrs Sweeney, you and Miss Beaver had better come with us."

"Here, Miss," a fireman said. "Put these boots on. You can return them when the storm is over."

"Oh, thank you," Addie Beaver said.

Anna had forgotten about Addie's high-buttoned shoes.

"Whatever you do, Anna, you are *not* to let go of my hand." Grandpa spoke firmly.

"Mr Jenson, would you mind if I held your other hand?" asked Mrs Sweeney.

"Not a bit," said Grandpa, "Anna, you take hold of Miss Beaver's hand. No one is to let go under *any* circumstances. Do you all understand?"

Anna had never heard Grandpa talk like that before. Was he frightened too?

They plunged into the deep snow, moving slowly along the south side of Fifteenth Street. The wind had piled the snow into huge drifts on the north side of the street.

When they reached Broadway, the wind was blowing up the avenue with the force of a hurricane. Telephone and telegraph wires were down. Thousands of them cut through the air like whips. If only they could reach the other side, Anna thought.

Carla Stevens

Anna, Grandpa and the big storm

Geography learning objectives

◆ To use atlases and globes, and other sources of information (2c, 2d).
◆ To describe what places are like (3d).
◆ To understand how weather affects the lives of people (3d, 4b).
◆ To recognise different weather conditions (4b).

Background notes

This story is based on the Great Blizzard of 1888 when winds blew at 75 mph and huge snowdrifts covered New York City.

Vocabulary

Thermometer, degrees, snowdrift, blizzard, Fahrenheit, Celsius, temperature.

Discussing the text

◆ Ask the class what the weather was like in the extract. What clues can they find in the text that tells them about the weather?
◆ Ask the children if this story is set in the past, the present or sometime in the future. Ask them to explain how they know this.
◆ Get the class to think about the characters in the text. Who are the main characters? How do they think each of them was feeling from the clues in the story?
◆ Discuss the children's experiences of severe weather. Have any of them experienced weather like that in the text? Talk about what they did and how they felt. If they have not had such an experience, get them to talk about how they think they would feel and react in such circumstances.
◆ *Anna had never heard Grandpa talk like that before.* Do the children think that he was frightened too? Are adults ever frightened? Do they think Grandpa was trying to hide it? Why?
◆ Can the children work out which country the story is set in and when? What phrases and words in the text tell us this? (*Broadway, high-buttoned shoes.*)

Geography activities

◆ Ask who in the class has been out in the snow. Ask them to describe what it is like. What sort of activities can we do in the snow? Explain that snow can be fun – but it can also be dangerous. Get the children to work in pairs to make lists of the good and bad aspects of snow.
◆ The weather in the story is a huge storm. Discuss with the children what we mean by a 'storm'. What kinds of storm can they think of? (Snow, rain, hail, but also look up 'force 10' on the beaufort wind scale and show them that this is defined as a 'storm' too.) How do storms affect us? Why are they so damaging? (They are all examples of extreme weather and it is difficult to prepare for true extremes.) Ask the children to select one type of storm and to draw a picture of a range of environments, such as a village, a woodland, the seaside, and describe how the place might be changed

or damaged by the storm.

◆ Discuss with the children the phrase *The thermometer says five degrees above zero…* How cold do they think 5°F is? What is the equivalent in Celsius? (-20°C.) How does a Fahrenheit thermometer differ from a Celsius one? Compare the two scales on a thermometer. As a class find out who uses °F and °C.

◆ Over a week or more, get the children to take and record the temperature in the school grounds (on a wall, out of the sun), and ask them to draw a graph of the results. They can extend this by looking up the temperatures of other places around the world (use the Internet or the weather reports in many daily newspapers). Where in the world has a temperature as cold as that in the story?

◆ Encourage the children to do some research on the Great Blizzard of 1888. What effect did it have on people and places in America? Get the children to write up their findings in the form of a short report for a newspaper.

Further literacy ideas

◆ Discuss with the class how snow changes the character of a place. Ask the children to make a list of words which describe the effect snow has on the way places look and feel (point out the quietness). Encourage the use of atmospheric and emotive words as well as straight description.

◆ Get the children to list the adjectives that are used to describe the weather and its effect on the characters in the story, for example *The wind roared and shrieked*. Choose another type of extreme weather (a rainstorm, high winds, a thunderstorm, a heat wave or drought) and ask the children to list suitable adjectives to describe it and its effect.

◆ Ask the children to write at least one synonym for each adjective they have written in the above activity. They can use a dictionary or thesaurus to help them if necessary. Ask them to substitute their synonyms for the adjectives in the text and discuss the difference these make to the effect.

◆ Ask the children to think about how the story might continue and get them to write an account of the characters' journey home. They could also write a preceding chapter to the text about events leading up to the extract.

◆ Take a number of sentences from the text and underline words randomly. Ask the children to say what class of word is underlined in each instance, for example noun, adjective, verb, and so on.

◆ Write a number of words from the text on a flip chart and asking the class for suggestions, underline the suffix in each, for example in *brushing*, *frightened*, *moving*, *huddled*. Ask the children if they can find other examples of suffixes in the text.

◆ Ask the children to identify all the verbs in the text, and to distinguish between those which are 'being' verbs and those which are 'doing' verbs.

◆ Ask the children to retell the story in the first person, as if they were either Anna or Grandpa.

◆ *Anna had never heard Grandpa talk like that before.* Ask the children to write a description of how they think Anna views her grandfather before and after the events in the story.

Where does water come from?

Genre
information
text –
diagram and
labels

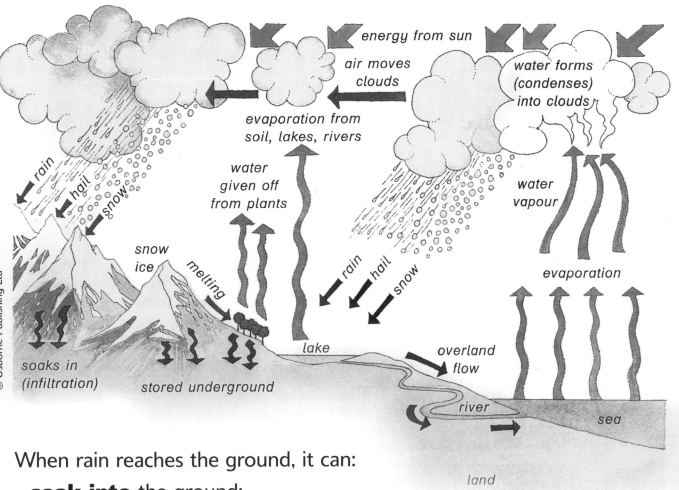

When rain reaches the ground, it can:

soak into the ground;

run off the surface;

evaporate;

but it does not disappear!

If it evaporates, it will fall again as **rain**, **hail** or **snow**.

What else might happen? Look at the picture.

Where does water come from?

Geography learning objectives

◆ To collect and record evidence (1b).

◆ To understand how to manage an environmental issue (2g, 6e).

◆ To understand and explain the processes of the water cycle (4b).

Background notes

The next three texts look at aspects of water in our environment. They can be used at a variety of levels and, although each can stand alone, they also complement each other well.

Vocabulary

Soak, run off, evaporate, rain, hail, snow, energy, condense, cloud, soil, lake, river, vapour, melt, infiltration, circular, overland flow.

Discussing the text

◆ Talk to the children about the way in which key information can be provided without the use of sentences and show them the text, focusing on how it conveys information. Discuss how the arrows are used in the diagram – how do they help the reader?

◆ Ask the class to describe where water comes from based on the information in the text.

◆ Can the children suggest why the term 'cycle' is used to describe the process in the text?

◆ Discuss the terms *diagram*, *heading*, *illustration* and *caption* with the children and make sure they can identify each within the text. Ask them to suggest why some of the words are printed in bold.

◆ Discuss the meaning of any unfamiliar words in the text, such as *infiltration*. Encourage the children to make a guess at their meaning by looking at the context in which they are used before helping them.

◆ Ask the children to suggest which category they think this text falls into – is it fiction or non-fiction?

Geography activities

◆ Get the children to follow the circular route around the diagram a number of times and to familiarise themselves with the cycle. Tell them to try starting at different points in the process each time.

◆ Ask: *Why is water so important to us?* Explore with the children how we use water at school, in the home and locally. Make a class list to display on the wall of all the different uses of water that the children can think of.

◆ Gather information about where your local water comes from and how much is used for different household functions. The children could write a letter to the water board for this information after discussing what they want to find out.

◆ Children can conduct a survey at home to determine how water is used and how much is used over a day, a week or a longer period. Results could be collected and put onto a suitable database.

◆ Ask the children what would happen if our water supply dwindled or was cut off for a period of time? Tell them that in parts of Spain in the summer months, water is only available for one or two hours each day. How would this rule change our lifestyles? Ask the children to draw up a set of rules for conserving water, or to draw a poster to encourage people to conserve water. They could try putting these into effect in their homes and report back on their success.

◆ Draw children's attention to any local conditions which might be appropriate – has there been a drought, or perhaps severe flooding in the area? How did this affect the local people? Get the children to choose a difficult weather scenario and to write a short newspaper report describing how people in the area coped with the situation.

Further literacy ideas

◆ Ask the children to sequence the events in the diagram, putting them into a list format.

◆ As a class, list all the vocabulary used in the diagram and sort the words into alphabetical order. Ask the children to choose ten of the words and compile a class glossary with them, discussing and agreeing on their meanings.

◆ Get the children to produce a simple flow diagram to represent an everyday procedure, such as getting dressed.

◆ Discuss the difference between fact and fiction with the children. Then ask them to find and record six facts from the text.

◆ Give the children some of the nouns from the text, such as *rain*, *lake*, *snow*, and ask them to list as many adjectives as possible to describe each, for example *water – warm*, *icy*, *frozen*, *clean*.

◆ Using the information in the text, get the children to write a series of sentences, or a couple of paragraphs, explaining where water comes from.

◆ Ask the children to use the text to write a list of questions and answers, for example *Where does energy come from? Energy comes from the sun.*

Water's progress

PHOTOCOPIABLE

Genre information text – diagram and captions

2. Some of the water vapour in the air **condenses** to form clouds.

3. When the water droplets in the cloud grow too big to float in the air, they fall as **rain**, **snow** or **hail**.

4. The rain runs off into streams or drains, or makes puddles (and evaporates again), or soaks into the ground. It runs into **rivers**, then back into lakes or the sea.

1. When water in seas, rivers and lakes is heated by the sun, it **evaporates** into the air.

When water comes out of the ground, it is called **a spring**. A river starts from here. It is called **the source**.

A larger river is formed from small, quick-flowing streams joining together. These smaller streams are called **tributaries**.

Sometimes valleys are winding, with hills jutting out on each side. These hills are called **spurs**.

Sometimes a river cuts a very steep-sided valley through hard rock. We call this valley **a gorge**.

Streams and small rivers make small **valleys**. Sometimes the water flows over the edge of hard rocks and creates **a waterfall**.

Where a river broadens out into a wide pool it forms **a lake**.

When a river has grown much bigger and reached flatter land, it begins to make wide, sweeping bends, called **meanders**.

If mudflats make islands in the river mouth, so that the river is divided into channels, the mouth becomes known as **a delta**.

Water plays a big part in making the land the shape it is. It **wears away** rock and carries away rock and soil to other places.

When rivers slow down, they drop the mud (silt) which they were carrying. This silt can form **sandbanks** or **mudflats**.

Where a river meets the sea is called **the mouth**. Sometimes it is called **an estuary**.

Water's progress

Geography learning objectives

◆ To use atlases and globes, and other sources of information (2c, 2d).

◆ To use appropriate geographical vocabulary to explain the main stages of the water cycle, and the changes that take place (2a, 4a, 4b).

◆ To identify key features of water in the landscape (6c).

Vocabulary

Water, water cycle, cloud, moisture, spring, rain, surface, spur, landscape, valley, mouth, tributary, delta, lake, waterfall, source, meander.

Discussing the text

◆ Discuss the layout of the text – how effective do the children think the presentation is? (Talk about how the illustration supports the captions.) Can they suggest alternative ways to present the information?

◆ Ask the children to think of other texts they know of that are set out in a similar format (find examples in text books or reference books, especially ones which show processes or a range of features on one picture). Revise the terms fiction and non-fiction with them and discuss the possible audience for this text. Where do the children think the extract came from? (It is from a non-fiction reference book.)

◆ Ask the children what they think the key words in the text are, for example, *evaporation, meanders*.

◆ Discuss and clarify any unfamiliar words in the text, such as *spur* or *tributary*.

Geography activities

◆ Recap with the children what the water cycle is. Which of the captions in the text explains the main stages? (They are numbered 1–4.) Which other labels identify processes in the water cycle? (The lake drying up.) Ask the children to summarise the key stages in a simplified flow chart.

◆ How many of the captions can be sequenced as a river story? Start with something like *When water comes out of the ground, it is called a spring. A river starts from here* and end at *Where the river meets the sea is called the mouth.* Get the children to write out different combinations as a piece of prose.

◆ How many examples of the river shaping the landscape are found in the captions? Can the children identify features in the illustration which have been formed by water action, such as a lake or a valley? The children can work in pairs or small groups to make a list of these, explaining how they have been created by the flow of water.

◆ Ask the children when they think rivers affect the landscape most rapidly. (In times of high flow.) How can we tell? (The colour of the water tells us

that it is carrying a lot of soil, or we see debris being carried along.) What do they notice in sloping fields or on sloping roads after heavy rain? (A lot of water runs off – often bringing soil from the fields.) Where do they think the water goes? (Down the drains – but ask them if they think it is lost or if it finds its way back into the water cycle.) Get the children to write up the main points from the discussion.

◆ What happens to the rain when it reaches the ground? Ask the children to make a list of all the things that *might* happen to it, such as dropping into a river, falling onto soil and soaking in, running off soil into a river, forming a puddle, and so on.

◆ Explain to the children that not all lakes are formed naturally. Some of them are man-made, in order to store water. Can they suggest how and why we store water? (For example, in reservoirs for human use, in dewponds for animals to drink from, in fish-ponds on a fish-farm.) Ask the children to make a list of ways that we use water, dividing them into 'practical' and 'other' categories (these might be decorative, such as a pond in a garden or an artificial lake).

◆ Are any of the other features in the text man-made? (The bridge, the lock.) Make a class list of features found along a river and divide them into natural and man-made features.

◆ Point out to the children that water also shapes the edge of the land (the coast). What evidence can they find of this in the picture? (Cliffs and a sandy beach.) Ask them to use reference books to find out about other seaside features related to water action. They should draw a picture of each feature they find, and write a caption explaining what the feature is and how it has been formed.

Further literacy ideas

◆ Use the text for the children to investigate comparative and superlative adjectives, for example *slower* and *slowest*.

◆ Ask the children to choose a part of the picture and set a story around it, for example by the waterfall or the mouth of the river. Make sure that they use some of the technical vocabulary from the text in their story.

◆ Compose a set of differentiated questions about the text for the children to complete, such as *What is a gorge?*

◆ Use the text as a basis from which to investigate compound words with the class, for instance *waterfall, sandbanks*.

◆ The children can use thesauruses to find alternatives for selected words in the text, for example *flows, winding, damaging*.

◆ Use the Look–Say–Cover–Write–Check method with the children for them to learn the spelling of some of the unfamiliar words in the text, such as *evaporates* and *condenses*.

◆ Get the children to convert the text into prose, organising the captions into paragraphs.

◆ Ask the children to use non-fiction books or the Internet to find out other facts about water. They can present their findings in an oral presentation or in written form for a display.

The river's song

Clear and cool, clear and cool,
By laughing shallow and dreaming pool;
Cool and clear, cool and clear,
By shining shingle and foaming weir;
Under the crag where the ouzel sings,
And the ivied wall where the church-bell rings,
Undefiled, for the undefiled,
Play by me, bathe in me, mother and child.

Dank and foul, dank and foul,
By the smoky town in its murky cowl;
Foul and dank, foul and dank,
By wharf and sewer and slimy bank;
Darker and darker the further I go,
Baser and baser the richer I grow;
Who dare sport with the sin-defiled?
Shrink from me, turn from me, mother and child.

Strong and free, strong and free,
The floodgates are open, away to the sea.
Free and strong, free and strong,
Cleansing my stream as I hurry along,
To the golden sands and the leaping bar,
And the taintless tide that awaits me afar,
As I lose myself in the infinite main
Like a soul that has sinned and is pardoned again.
Undefiled, for the undefiled,
Play by me, bathe in me, mother and child.

Charles Kingsley

The river's song

Geography learning objectives

◆ To collect and record evidence (1b).

◆ To use appropriate geographical vocabulary (2a).

◆ To use atlases and maps (2c).

◆ To explain how and why places change (3e).

◆ To recognise how places fit into a wider context (3g).

Background notes

This poem traces the course – and quality – of a river in Victorian times. It provides opportunities to investigate the river through its course, the uses of a river and issues of water quality and pollution.

Vocabulary

Clear, cool, shallow, pool, shingle, weir, crag, dank, foul, murky, wharf, sewer, bank, floodgates, sands, bar, tide.

Discussing the text

◆ Discuss the main idea behind the poem with the children. Do they know of any other poems about rivers and pollution? Look at and discuss these together.

◆ Establish the pattern that the poem follows – the use of a repeating line in each verse. Discuss its effect on the reader or listener with the children.

◆ There are a number of unfamiliar words in the text, such as *ouzel* and *cowl*. Before asking the children to look them up, discuss possible meanings for them by looking at their context.

◆ Look at the rhythm of the poem with the children – does it differ in different verses? Why do they think this is?

◆ *Like a soul that has sinned and is pardoned again.* Discuss the author's use of this simile. Can the children think of other similes, or metaphors, to describe parts of the river's journey?

Geography activities

◆ Identify with the children which parts of the river are described in the poem (source and upper reach, middle and lower reach, lower reach and estuary respectively, in the three verses).

◆ Ask the children to draw a diagram to show the river's progress from source to mouth, and to label all the parts and features to be found in each section. They should start with features mentioned in the text, then move on to suggest others (they could use reference books to extend their list).

◆ What else might the river be used for during its course?

(Work activities, leisure activities, drainage for agricultural land, irrigation.) Make a class list on a flip chart of possible uses of the river.

◆ Discuss with the class the sorts of pollution that might occur along the full stretch of the river. Is industrial pollution the only type? (Other types of pollution include litter, dead animals in the upper reaches, agricultural run-off in the middle reaches and seaside or port pollution at the mouth, for example.)

◆ In groups, ask the children to find out what the major rivers of the UK, Europe and the world are. Each group can be allocated different areas to research. Ask them to mark the main rivers on wall maps, with each river labelled with its name and the main points of interest about it. Which rivers are most in danger of being polluted?

◆ How do leisure activities contribute to river pollution? Ask the children to make a table of leisure activities and their good and bad impacts on the waterways, for example a good point about boating is that it earns money for the boat companies, but the fuel could pollute the river.

◆ Ask the children to investigate their local river or stream. How clean or polluted is it? Have there been any cases of pollution lately? (See local papers.) Visit it and make a class inventory of the pollutants which occur even in a 'clean' river.

Further literacy ideas

◆ Point out some examples of alliteration from the poem, such as *shining shingle*. Supply the children with other words from the poem, such as *bank, sea, stream*, and get them to write alliterative descriptions for them.

◆ Identify some of the strong adjectives used by the author (such as *dank, foul, taintless*). Ask the children to experiment by replacing a few of them. Can they change the overall effect of the poem by using 'softer' words? (For instance, *dirty, smelly, clean* instead.)

◆ Ask the children to write a paragraph for each verse of the poem in prose, explaining what the author is saying about the river. Ensure they use paragraphs correctly and ask them to comment on the difference in punctuation in both formats.

◆ Ask the children to find rhyming words which have different spelling combinations in the poem, such as *foul* and *cowl*, *clear* and *weir*. Devise spelling strategies that would help less able children learn how to spell these words.

◆ Ask the children if they know which person the poem is written in (the first person), and how they can tell (*Play by me, bathe in me…*). Ask them to change this to the third person.

◆ Get the children to choose another feature of the landscape, such as a park, a city or a village near a busy road, and to write a poem in a similar style.

◆ Revise word classification with the children. They can highlight all the nouns, verbs, adjectives and so on, in different colours.

◆ Revise synonyms with the class and get them to individually 'translate' the poem, by replacing some of the less familiar words with those used more commonly today. The children can read their revised version out to the rest of the class.

CHAPTER 3

Human geography

Like physical geography, human geography looks at the processes of change and the development of places as generated by people, in contrast to the 'natural' processes which occur in physical geography. Children will learn to recognise common patterns of development in different places, and come to understand that there are similar forces at work generating change and development as in physical geography studies.

In the study of human geography, children will look at various types of settlement, both large and small, and at how they have grown or changed over time. They will also study the provision of services, such as shops and transport, and the jobs that people do (manufacturing, providing raw materials or transporting and selling goods) and how this is reflected in the settlement itself.

They will learn to recognise the features and patterns related to different types of settlement, including the way that different places are linked together. Patterns such as growth on the edge of settlements, or the redevelopment of the centre, will be recognised, or the way that transport links affect places (motorways and bypasses, for instance, may well have a profound affect on a place. Near a motorway junction there may be a lot of new development, both industrial and residential, whereas the lack of a nearby motorway junction may mean that a once-busy small town is now much quieter than before, with many shops and small businesses closing down).

The selected texts in this chapter largely bring out aspects of life in different settlements. The 'Town transect' and 'Town and country' texts identify some of the common features of different settlements and indicate the parallels between them.

What's in a name?

Genre
information
text

When we look at a map the names of places can tell us quite a lot about the place – as long as we can work out what the meaning is.

In some places, people discovered that the local water was good for their health. Many of these places now have names with *spa* added, such as *Bath Spa*.

We can even find clues about people who lived there in the past and where they came from – if the name they gave it is the one in use today.

Here are some parts of place names that give us clues:

Name part	Meaning	People
Aber-	rivermouth	
Llan-	church	Celts
Pen-	top, end	(before the Romans)
Tre-, Trev-	village	
-caster	camp, fort	
-cester	camp, fort	Romans
-chester	camp, fort	
-port	harbour, gate	
-borough	fortified place	
-bridge	bridge	
-bury	fortified place	
-den	pasture in wood	
-ford	ford (river crossing)	Angles and Saxons
-ham	village	
-hurst	copse	
-ing	the people of	
-ley	clearing	
-ton	village	
-by	homestead	
-thorpe	settlement	Scandinavians
-thwaite	clearing	(Norsemen)
-toft	clearing	

What's in a name?

Geography learning objectives

◆ To observe and record evidence from maps (1b, 2c).

◆ To analyse evidence, express their views about reasons for settlement (1c, 4b).

◆ To identify and describe where places are and what they are like (3a, 3c).

◆ To describe a variety of patterns of settlement (4a, 6d).

Background notes

This extract looks at the interesting roots and origins of names of places found on Ordnance Survey (OS) maps. It gives a present-day geographical perspective to the study of invaders and settlers in the history National Curriculum.

Vocabulary

Celts, Romans, Anglo-Saxons, Scandinavians, haven, pasture, clearing, settlement, homestead, clearing, fortified, pasture, copse.

Discussing the text

◆ Discuss the title of the text – what do the children think it might be about? Show them the very first sentence of text on an OHP, *When we look at a map, the names of places can tell us quite a lot about the place…* Ask the children to explain what they think this means. Can they think of the names of any places that represent the places themselves, for example Ross-on-Wye being near the Wye river?

◆ Talk about the fact that certain place names have certain meanings. Read the second sentence of the text with the children. Do the children know what sort of place would be found with the word *bay* or *cove* in it? Do they know of any other place names that have particular meanings? (Some of them may have heard of a ford being a river crossing.)

◆ Read through the introductory text in paragraphs and ask the children for examples already known to them of places that end with *Spa*, and then other examples from the list of place names and meanings given.

◆ Discuss the pronunciation of the words on the list, such as *Llan-*, *-borough* and *-thwaite*.

◆ Discuss the groups of people associated with the different place names, such as the Celts. Do the children know where these people came from? Do they know what countries make up Scandinavia? Can they think why people who came from this region are sometimes called Norsemen?

◆ Ask the children to suggest possible audiences for the text. Who might want to know about the origins of place names? (Historians and archaeologists.)

Geography activities

◆ Discuss with the children the composition and significance of names using their own surnames as a starting point. For instance, Henderson would possibly mean the son of Hender, Smith could give a clue to what was at one time someone's job. Develop this to talk about place names and how these can also tell us something about a place, and possibly the early settlers there.

◆ Revise any previous work done on settlers in a history unit. Look at the early waves of settlers, such as the Romans, Angles and Saxons, and the Normans, who arrived and changed the lives of the British, or Celtic, peoples. Where did these settlers come from and why? Look at an atlas to see their origins and the possible journeys they had to make. Which coast of Britain would they have been most likely to land on?

◆ Use some extracts from OS maps which will allow the children to identify the names of places where there is evidence of early settlers. Some areas which are less built up will be more useful, such as Lincolnshire or East Anglia. Urban areas are more likely to have lost their original names, which may have been subsumed into more industrial or modern names.

◆ Give the children copies of a local map and ask them to analyse the geographical influences which have helped to form the names of places. Sometimes these can include people's names, local raw materials or other languages, such as French. Physical features, such as hills, valleys or bays are common. Ask the children to write a report on their findings.

◆ Encourage the children to look at some of the small settlements on the local map and try to identify some of the original reasons why the place was chosen for a settlement, for example a river-crossing point, the fact that it was far from a flood plain, or near water supplies or shelter. When the children are used to looking for these mainly physical reasons they can try the exercise on more densely populated maps, where more complex reasons for settlements are often found.

◆ After discussing the reasons identified for settlement patterns with the children, ask them to create their own settlement map. Give them a list of specific features to plot, including things such as a village, woodland, some farms, a river and an area of hilly ground. Tell them to name as many of the features as they can with suitable names. Remind the children that all roads go somewhere – they rarely end in a field!

Further literacy ideas

◆ Give the children one or more of the letter patterns shown in the 'Name part' column of the text, such as -bury, and ask them to brainstorm a list of words that contain this letter pattern.

◆ Use the words under the 'Meaning' column as the basis for a spelling exercise. Revise the Look–Cover–Say–Write–Check method with the class.

◆ Ask the children to use a map and find an example for each word in the 'Meaning' column. They can then create a dictionary or a glossary, of word meanings and examples (such as Ford – river crossing – Shalford).

◆ Ask the children to write a mystery story set in one of the places described in the text, for example a clearing in a wood, or involving a river crossing.

◆ Ask the children to write full sentences using the information in the text, for example A place name that contains the word part -borough may have been a fortified place in Anglo-Saxon times.

◆ Get the children to imagine they can travel back to a time when either the Romans, Anglo-Saxons or Norsemen were around, and to write a story set in those times. Encourage the children to use non-fiction reference books to help them set the scene for their story. They could choose a character, such as a Viking chief, and complete a character profile before they start their story.

Genre
information text in a persuasive leaflet/travel brochure

Europa©

Set in the amazing Minnesotan Lake district, Europa brings to life Europe under one roof!

Visit the Colosseum, listen to the chimes of Big Ben, gasp at the size of Notre Dame and be amazed at the Parthenon – all in a single day! But yet Europa offers people enough excitement to keep everyone amused for a week.

Try your hand at blowing the gigantic alpenhorn or playing the bagpipes; or visit the playground where children can squeeze through the enormous Swiss Cheese.

All countries are linked by a miniature alpine railway, which allows you to visit all the sights and stop off where you please.

Hop on! Hop off! Tickets valid all day!

Hotel Alpenhorn

The Hotel Alpenhorn boasts comfortable accommodation in accordance with the European theme. Every room has a double bed, with additional bunk beds for the children. Each room has full en suite facilities, and digital TV.

© IKON Imaging

Bambini Bargains

☆ Special offer for 2–11 year olds *
☆ Free admission to Europa [1]
☆ Free accommodation [2]
☆ Free entry to historical pageant [3]
☆ Photograph with a European character of choice [4]

© 2001, Comstock, Inc

The indoor boulevard cafés offer a superb range of food to satisfy all taste buds. Children's menus are also available.

For the little Europeans, there is a fabulous playground with mountains to climb, glaciers to slide down and a cable-car ropeway to conquer, not to mention the forest of cheeses to hide away in.

Free car parking for customers.

☆ Eat continental ☆

Eat in a different country every night. Books of meal tickets can be purchased in advance, changeable in the Greek Taverna, Café Parisienne, Pizzeria Roma, Waffle-Bar Bruxelles and Tony's Fish & Chip Shop. Why not try the paella in the Restaurante Espagna, or even the Brockwürst in the Berliner Würsthaus?

© Photodisc, Inc

[1] 1 Oct to 30 April only.
[2] 1 Dec to 28 Feb only.
[3] Must be booked in advance.
[4] List of characters available on request.

Europa

Geography learning objectives

◆ To express their own views about places such as Europa (1d).

◆ To use appropriate geographical vocabulary (2a).

◆ To use atlases, maps, photographs and plans (2c, 2d).

◆ To describe what Europa is like and why people go there (3a, 3c, 3d, 3g, 7b).

◆ To recognise how places compare with one another (3f, 3g).

Background notes

This text is based around the imaginary 'Europa' theme park in Minnesota, USA, about 225 km (140 miles) north-west of Minneapolis. (Minnesota is known as the 'State of 10 000 lakes'.) The text enables you to explore ideas of perceptions and stereotypes of different countries with the children.

Vocabulary

Colosseum, Parthenon, bagpipes, Swiss, alpine, theme park, accommodation, pageant, en suite, admission, boulevard, cable car, glacier, continental, European.

Discussing the text

◆ Read the opening paragraph of the text and experiment with reading the words with different expression and intonation. Discuss with the children how this affects the impact of the text on the reader. Ask different children to take turns in reading this paragraph in different ways, for example quickly, slowly and miserably. Discuss what the intention of the brochure is (to persuade the reader that they want to visit this place). Discuss what words are used to try and persuade people to visit Europa (for example, *be amazed*). Ask the children if they think the language in the brochure is effective – are they persuaded?

◆ Talk about the overall layout of the text – what fonts are used to try and catch the reader's eye and are they effective? Which font do the children like best? Talk about the footnotes for the 'Bambini bargains' section. Why is this text in small print? Is it important information? Do the children think it is fair to write this information in this way?

◆ Read through the factual information, such as that about the Hotel Alpenhorn. Pick out the key words with the children and discuss any particularly persuasive words or phrases used to try and tempt the reader.

◆ Discuss the copyright symbol on the title of the brochure and what it is used for it – have the children seen this symbol used before? Where have they seen it?

Geography activities

◆ Discuss with the children where they think Europa is. What are the clues? Make a list of the clues that it is in America. Where is the one place which actually states where it is located? Talk about theme parks in general. Have any of the children visited one? If so, where and what was it like?

HUMAN GEOGRAPHY

◆ Look at a map of America with the class and find Minnesota. Discuss its location in relation to the rest of the country. Where do the children think visitors are likely to come from? What is the difference between travelling there for example, from Texas or from Ontario in Canada? If they were travelling there from another state in America, which roads might they travel on? (A freeway.)

◆ Discuss the themes of the park. Which characteristics of Europe are portrayed? Do the children think that Europa represents life today in Europe?

◆ Discuss with the children what we mean by *stereotypes* and identify those in the text. Ask: *Are any stereotypes useful or realistic? Do they help us understand people and how they live?* (No, even though there may be a grain of truth in a stereotype, they act as a barrier to understanding and respect for other cultures.)

◆ Either with a partner or in a small group, ask the children to design their own version of the text, using the characteristics of another country or continent. They can research their subject by using books from the school library or a suitable Internet site.

◆ Show the children a brochure of another theme park or country park. Discuss the features and activities provided. Ask the children to plan a day out for a family, and get them to consider factors such as how they will travel there, and what they will see and do. They should plan a route there for the driver of a car to follow from the school.

◆ Ask the children to carry out a survey at school to find out information about theme parks. Tell them to ensure they tailor their questions to gain the information they want, for instance finding out how people travel there, what they liked most and least, what the main attraction of going there was and would they go again? Once the results are in, create a simple database so that each child can enter their information. Then, as a class, analyse the results. What conclusions can be drawn?

Further literacy ideas

◆ Get the children to advertise their own theme park. Ask them to pick a theme, and to write an introductory paragraph in a similar style to that in the text. They may want to start this exercise by brainstorming a list of persuasive words or phrases that they can use.

◆ Discuss critics and the idea that they write reviews of places to stay or restaurants to eat in. Ask the children to imagine that they have visited the Hotel Alpenhorn and to write a review about it for the local newspaper.

◆ Focus on the difference between fact and fiction. In a guided writing lesson, give the children a section of the text and ask them to underline or make a list of any facts they can find. Then compare these with some of the opinions stated in the text.

◆ Use the text as a starting point for letter writing. Ask the children to write a letter to the Hotel Alpenhorn imagining that they have recently stayed there. They could either compliment the hotel on some of its features, or make a complaint about something that they expected from having read the brochure but were not satisfied with.

◆ Ask the children to write down examples of proper nouns in the text and examples of ordinary nouns. This activity could be extended to cover other parts of grammar, such as adjectives or adverbs.

◆ Give the children a list of statements based on the text and ask them to write down whether they think they are true or false.

❧ ❧ The Café Dog ❧ ❧

Genre

*fictional
extract from
a longer
story/novel*

The seaside resort of Multon is not very big. It has a short pier with an amusement arcade and a kiosk at the end selling souvenirs, ice cream, rock and candy floss. There are also a putting green, a crazy golf course, tennis courts, a paddling pool for toddlers, some guest houses, a few shops, two pubs and a café. The main reason people go to Multon is not so much for these modest attractions but because of the town's situation. It lies at one end of a broad bay, sheltered from the wind, and the sea around it is comfortably warm throughout the summer. Bathing there is a delight and, at the height of the season, Multon is thronged with visitors. There are boat trips across the bay and also to the island of Clany, about half an hour distant. Only a small number of people live on the island and most of them are monks, hidden away in the monastery which has been established on Clany for centuries.

The esplanade at Multon follows the curve of the bay and is lined by fisherman's cottages, most of which are now converted into shops or guest houses. Near the entrance to the pier, some years ago, one of the cottages was turned into the Seagull Café. This was owned for thirty years by the same proprietors, Mr and Mrs Clements. Every morning during the season, the café door was opened by Mr Clements at exactly half-past eight. Not to let in the first customers of the day, because there were never any around so early, but to let out a little white rough-haired terrier called Zoe. Zoe was a West Highland White, a Christmas present one year from Mr and Mrs Clements' son to his parents. She was rather an unlooked-for Christmas present since the owners of the Seagull Café were not too happy about keeping a dog in a place where food was served all day. So they decided that during the hours when the café was open, Zoe would have to be put outside. And when it was closed, or if the weather turned very cold, she would only be allowed into their living quarters above the café.

Zoe got quite used to this and usually made a beeline for the steps leading down from the promenade to the beach, especially in wet weather when she would shelter under the pier. She liked to roam around the shingle exploring the new scents her inquisitive nose picked up each day. She made friends with another dog, Bertram who was often to be found on the beach too. But whereas Zoe was still young and full of energy, Bertram was old and spent a lot of time sleeping. Then she would leave him and wander off on her own. It was because of this, more than anything else, that one September, late in the season, they embarked on an adventure which was to have consequences neither of them expected.

Colin Dann

The café dog

Geography learning objectives

◆ To analyse and record evidence (1b, 1c).

◆ To use secondary sources of information (2d).

◆ To identify and describe what places are like (3a).

◆ To describe and explain how places are similar to and different from other places in the same country and elsewhere in the world (3f).

◆ To understand how settlements differ and change, including why they differ in size and character (6d).

Vocabulary

Multon, pier, amusement arcade, kiosk, souvenirs, putting green, guest house, attractions, situation, bathing, esplanade, bay, proprietor, shingle.

Discussing the text

◆ Focus on each paragraph in turn and ask the children what the main focus of each is.

◆ Draw the children's attention to the phrase *rather an unlooked-for Christmas present*. What do they think it means? What is the difference between *unlooked-for*, *unwanted* and *unexpected*?

◆ Discuss the relationship between Zoe and Mr and Mrs Clements with the class. How does their relationship link to the slogan, 'A dog is for life, not just for Christmas'?

◆ Multon is *thronged with visitors* in the summer. How do the children think this would affect the resort? Discuss what it is like out of season and the term *seasonal*. How will people who live there be affected by this?

◆ Talk with the children about the jobs that are identified in the text. Are there any which are implied but not specified? (Such as a shopkeeper, guest-house proprietor.) How many of these jobs are seasonal?

◆ What do the children think that life would be like on the island of Clany? How would this differ from life on the mainland?

◆ Multon is described as having *modest attractions*. Discuss this phrase with the children. How justified do they think the use of this phrase is from the description of the place in the text?

Geography activities

◆ Using the text, make a class list of Multon's features on a flip chart, under the following headings: 'landscape', 'weather', 'tourist facilities/activities'. Discuss how the place might have changed or developed over the years.

◆ Discuss the sort of jobs that people in Multon might do. Are they full-time jobs all the year round? Would some of the people have two part-time jobs due to the seasonal nature of the area? How would this affect the way the local people live? Get the children to write two parallel descriptions of Multon – one at the height of the season and one out of season.

◆ Ask the children to use the information in the text to draw a sketch map of the area, showing the position of Multon in relation to the bay. They should label the features of the coastline, including the island of Clany.

◆ Give the children OS maps of coastal areas so that they can locate similar seaside resorts. Working in small groups, ask them to compare the features of Multon with those of other seaside resorts. They could also use tourist information brochures, and pictures of resorts in other countries, to make a chart listing similarities and differences between Multon and other resorts. Ask them to write an explanation alongside each difference.

◆ Discuss the importance of climate and position for a resort such as Multon with the children. What words in the text will help with this? (Look for words which give clues about the weather in summer and how sheltered the town is.)

◆ The children can work in groups to put together a tourist brochure for the seaside resort of Multon. They could use ICT methods to create the overall design and to produce the brochure.

Further literacy ideas

◆ Ask the children to imagine Zoe is writing about her arrival at the Seagull Café, and to write an account from her point of view in the first person. Suggest the children use the information from the text to help with setting, characters, and so on.

◆ Get the children to write a review for the local paper about the seaside resort of Multon. They should produce a copy and redraft it, using a word-processor if possible, so that they can experiment with layout and typefaces.

◆ Suggest the children continue the story. What happened to Zoe and Bertram? What were the consequences that neither of them expected?

◆ The children can use dictionaries to record the meaning of a set of words as they are used in the text, such as *modest, thronged, inquisitive, consequence*.

◆ As a follow-up activity, the children could use a thesaurus to find alternative words to those investigated above.

◆ Read the children a passage from another book by Colin Dann. What similarities in the style of the writer can they identify?

◆ Ask the children to design and write their own advertisement for Multon to be aired on television. Alternatively, they could write a script for a 'Wish you were here'-style TV report on Multon.

◆ Explain to the children that some people object to dogs being allowed on the beach. As a class, list the arguments for and against their being allowed on the beach on the flip chart. Ask the children to think about it from the point of view of the dogs, their owners, other visitors and the proprietors of local amenities or stalls.

The Red Umbrella – Part One

Genre
story from another culture

Obed and his family lived in a township a few miles outside the town. Most of the fathers and the young people who lived in the township worked in the town. They worked in the town shops and the town banks and the town factories. Obed's father worked on the railway, in the shunting yard, helping to unload the trains. Each morning he went to work on the town bus with the other people who worked in the town, and he came home on the bus in the evening.

Around the township was a large, high wire fence. One year, before there was a fence, a leopard had come into the town and had eaten some of Obed's mother's ducks. The township people had been very frightened, so a fence had been built around the township to stop the wild animals coming close to the houses and to stop the children straying into the bundu. The bundu was the land around the township which was thick with trees and bushes and high grasses. Monkeys swung about in the trees and there were butterflies as big as your two hands put together. There were also wild pigs and snakes, and Obed and his sister were told never to go out of the township and into the bundu, as it was too dangerous.

Outside the township houses there were deep ditches, called storm drains, running the length of the streets. At the end of October the rains started and it rained every single day until March. It would be hot at mid-day, but by the middle of the afternoon the sky would become black, and the thunder would start and the lightning crack, and down would come the rain in large, heavy drops, beating hard on the ground and bouncing as high as Obed's knees. Usually Obed was home before the rain started, but his sister was often caught in the afternoon rain. The water would run down the roofs and onto the ground like huge waterfalls, and run away into the storm drains, down the streets and into a big lake near the gate of the township. This lake was called the dambo, and Molly and Obed were allowed to go with their friends to the dambo, where they took off their clothes and swam in the clear water and made rafts with wood and old tin cans. However, when it rained Mrs Band would not let Molly and Obed near the storm drains. Each house had a bridge of paving stones at the end of its pathway, over the drain, so that they could cross to the road. Obed loved to drop wood or rubbish from the little bridge into the storm drain and watch the swift-flowing water carry it away, but his mother used to shout, "Obed, keep away. Many's the child who has been swept away and never seen again."

In the hot dry season, however, the storm drains were empty and dusty and the home of small lizards, called skinks. Obed used to race these skinks by lining them up and poking them on the tail with a stick, but they often all ran in different directions or hid under the nearest stone, so he became tired of them quickly. Obed much preferred the lizards called geckos, which lived in the corners of the bedroom ceiling and ate all the mosquitoes. Obed's bedroom windows had netting across them all the year round to keep the mosquitoes out, but they still found their way into the house, and Obed was glad that the geckos ate them all up, as they were such a nuisance, buzzing around as he was trying to go to sleep.

Valerie Lapthorne

The Red Umbrella – Part One

Geography learning objectives

◆ To ask geographical questions (1a).

◆ To analyse evidence and draw conclusions (1c).

◆ To identify and explain what places are like and the different views about places (1d, 3a).

◆ To describe and explain how and why places are similar and different (3f).

◆ To understand more about a locality in a less economically developed country (6b).

Background notes

This story is set in Zambia and tells the story of Obed and his family in a township. The title refers to the gift Obed wants to buy his mother for her birthday as he overhears her saying to her neighbour that it would be nice to have a big umbrella to cover her when the rainy season comes. It provides a vivid account of life there. It also allows children to be able to relate to it, and to recognise the similarities with their own lives as well as the differences.

Vocabulary

Township, factories, leopard, bundu, monkeys, butterflies, dangerous, lightning, thunder, waterfall, storm drain, lizards, skinks, geckos, mosquitoes, nuisance.

Discussing the text

◆ Discuss the title of the story with the children. Do they have any suggestions as to what the story might be about? Read the first paragraph through with them –are there any surprises? Can they think of a reason why the story is called 'The Red Umbrella'? Read the extract all the way through and ask if there are any more ideas about the title. (The rain in paragraph three.)

◆ Discuss the word *township*. Have the children heard of this word before? Do they know what it is? Talk about the context in which the children may have heard this word? Do they know where in the world has townships?

◆ Discuss with the children where they think the story is set. Ask what clues they can pick up to help them, such as the living conditions described in the last paragraph. Write down their suggestions on a flip chart before discussing that it is set in East Africa. Show them where this is on an atlas and a globe.

◆ Read the first line of the second paragraph to the children, *Around the township was a large, high wire fence.* Why do the children think there needs to be a wire fence around the township? List any reasons that they suggest on the flip chart. Then read the remainder of the second paragraph with the children. Were they surprised? Discuss any differences between the children's reasons and what is actually written in the story.

◆ Talk about the rains described in the third paragraph. Do the children know of any parts of the world where there is continuous heavy rain for long periods of time, as described in the text? Talk about the term *monsoon*. Discuss what the children think it would be like to live in these conditions. How is it similar or different to the conditions that the children live in themselves? What would the advantages and disadvantages of such conditions be?

Geography activities

◆ Ask the children to draw a series of pictures to illustrate the place in the story and to label them. Talk a little about the type of houses which might be found there and what sort of building materials might be used. It is also important to identify the things which will not be there – the modern features of their own school area, for example.

◆ Ask the children to draw similar landscape scenes for their own local area, and again to label the main features. They can then identify the things which will be the same in both sets of pictures. This will help to heighten their awareness of the similarities, rather than the differences.

◆ Read the paragraph about the rainstorm again. Discuss with the children how this is different from rain in their area. Point out that rain in the UK can happen at any time and often the skies are overcast and rain falls steadily. At other times we have thunderstorms. Ask them to describe how this differs from the rain in the story.

◆ Using an atlas, identify the continent of Africa with the class. Ask the children to make a list of all the things they know about Africa. This can vary tremendously, but often concepts such as hot, deserts, wildlife or tropical forests will surface. It is then important to relate it, for example, to Europe, where very diverse features and climate exist within one land mass. Talk about the various regions of Africa and find the Equator. Show pictures of the different regions and play some African music to the children. Make sure you include some pictures of the city skyscrapers of Durban or Johannesburg, to ensure that they see a balance in the types of places that exist in the country.

◆ Ask the children to research some of the wildlife, insects and vegetation mentioned in the text. Make a display of their findings. Discuss the good and bad effects of these on humans, for example the dangers of wildlife, or the spread of diseases such as malaria or sleeping sickness.

◆ After reading the information in the text again, ask the children to identify all the features in each paragraph and to use these to create a labelled map of the district. This may be extended to include the township, factory/industrial area, railways, bundu/forest, the lake and the bridge.

Further literacy ideas

◆ Ask the children to write a story about when the leopard came into the township and ate the ducks. They should write the story from the viewpoint of one of the township people. Before they start, encourage them to build up a profile of the character and to then include these characteristics in their story, making reference to the way they think the character would behave in that situation.

◆ Brainstorm words with the class to describe the rain in the text. They can use these to write a poem entitled 'From October to March' about how the rains fall every single day. The children should focus on rhythm and repetition to recreate the sound of rain.

◆ Ask the children to write a short story based on a visit to the dambo by Molly and Obed. Tell them to imagine the rains start and one character wants to stay and play, but the other feels they should follow their mother's instructions and leave. Ask them to write about the conflict between the characters, and to concentrate on speech marks and the correct punctuation to separate speakers.

◆ *Many's the child who has been swept away and never seen again.* Using this as an example of a moral to a story, get the children to write a story explaining the consequences of not heeding advice.

◆ Get the children to pick out all or some of the adjectives used in the text. They should put them into groups according to whether they describe people, places or weather.

◆ Give out some non-fiction reference books and ask the children to find out more about some of the wildlife mentioned in the story, such as geckos and lizards. They can make their own class reference book with the information they find.

The Red Umbrella – Part Two

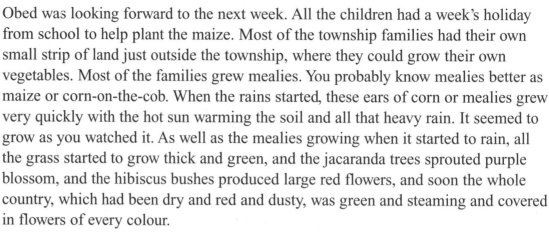

Genre
story from another culture

Obed was looking forward to the next week. All the children had a week's holiday from school to help plant the maize. Most of the township families had their own small strip of land just outside the township, where they could grow their own vegetables. Most of the families grew mealies. You probably know mealies better as maize or corn-on-the-cob. When the rains started, these ears of corn or mealies grew very quickly with the hot sun warming the soil and all that heavy rain. It seemed to grow as you watched it. As well as the mealies growing when it started to rain, all the grass started to grow thick and green, and the jacaranda trees sprouted purple blossom, and the hibiscus bushes produced large red flowers, and soon the whole country, which had been dry and red and dusty, was green and steaming and covered in flowers of every colour.

However, there was a lot of work to be done before the rains started. Father had part of the week off work and on Monday morning they got ready to go to their strip of land. Mrs Banda made them a good breakfast from the flour which is made from the mealies and called mealie-meal. To make mealie-meal, Mrs Banda and Molly used to gather all the corn from the mealies when they were ripe. They dried them in the sun and then pounded the corn in a big wooden bowl. The bowl was so big that it stood on the ground, and Mrs Banda and Molly stood by the bowl with heavy poles. These poles were worn smooth with many years of use, and they were used to pound the corn in the bowl into flour. First Molly thudded her pole into the corn and then Mrs Banda. They sang as they worked and beat time with their poles in the bowl. When they had finished they tossed the flour in the air from flat baskets, and all the pieces of cornshell blew away leaving the flour on the basket. They stored the flour in sacks ready to make into mealie-meal porridge, which they had at each meal.

Molly fed the ducks and collected the eggs and they all set off. Father and Obed carried the hoes, Molly some mealie-meal porridge in a bowl upon her head, and Mrs Banda carried baby James on her back and a bowl of stew on her head for their mid-day meal, and the basket of eggs. On the way out they stopped at the shop and Mrs Banda left her eggs with the shopkeeper and Mr Banda bought a jug of beer to take with them. Many of their neighbours were also heading for the fields with their hoes, and sometimes someone would start a song and the long walk to the fields passed quite quickly.

The sun was already hot when they started work and by mid-morning it was very hot indeed, but they carried on turning over the dry, dusty red earth and breaking up the lumps and digging out the big stones. Mrs Banda put James on the ground to crawl around and play with the stones while she gathered dry twigs for the lunchtime cooking fire. Suddenly Mrs Banda screamed and stood very still. In gathering up some dried twigs she had disturbed a puff adder, which had been sheltering from the sun, and it reared its head up and was hissing and its puffed-out head was swaying backwards and forwards. Mr Banda leapt across the field and brought his heavy hoe down across the head of the puff adder, and it twitched and lay still. Mrs Banda, Molly and Obed looked at the dead snake with its pretty green and silver markings. It was strange that such a beautiful creature should have such a poisonous bite.

Valerie Lapthorne

The Red Umbrella – Part Two

Geography learning objectives

◆ To ask geographical questions (1a).

◆ To analyse and record evidence (1c).

◆ To use appropriate fieldwork techniques (2b).

◆ To identify and describe what places are like (3a).

◆ To study a small-scale area in a less economically developed locality (6b, 7a).

Background notes

This extract follows on from the previous one and is set in the same place. It shows aspects of life in the township and the methods of farming carried out by one of the families living there. It provides an opportunity for children to recognise the number of similarities which actually exist between their culture and the one in the story.

Vocabulary

Maize, mealies, vegetables, jacaranda, blossom, hibiscus, cornshell, hoe, puff adder, beautiful, poisonous.

Discussing the text

◆ Read the first two sentences of this extract with the children. Why do they think that Obed looked forward to this particular activity? Discuss what sort of things the children look forward to when they have a week off school. How are these activities similar or different? Talk about how the differences in these activities are linked to the environment in which the children live. Ask the children to imagine that they live in the township and to think about why Obed looks forward to this.

◆ Read through the passage with the children until the word *mealie* is mentioned. Do the children have any idea what mealies are? Before reading on to the explanation of what mealies are, can the children guess, given what they know about the setting for this extract? List the children's ideas on a flip chart and then continue reading the passage.

◆ Discuss the description of mealie as *It seemed to grow as you watched it*. Why do the children think that the author says this? Is it actually true? What is the author trying to impress upon the reader?

◆ Discuss the process of making mealie-meal. How does this compare to the breakfast that the children are used to? Discuss any alternatives to their normal breakfast that the children may have experienced when visiting friends or relatives at home or abroad.

◆ *It was strange that such a beautiful creature should have such a poisonous bite*. Discuss this final sentence with the children. What point is the author trying to make?

Geography activities

◆ Discuss with the children the concept of growing vegetables in the garden. Who grows their own at home? Are there any allotments in the area? Where do their families get their vegetables from? Talk about the types of vegetables found in the local supermarket. How can we buy vegetables? (Fresh, tinned, dried, frozen.) What are the differences between these ways of processing them?

◆ Ask the children to draw an annotated sketch to show the Bandas' way of life. This can be one composite picture, or a series of pictures, to show the variety of landscapes and the activities mentioned in the extract. They could then draw a similar series of annotated sketches to illustrate their own daily lives.

◆ As a class, make a list of all the foods the Bandas eat. How many of these do we eat? (Maize, corn on the cob, porridge, eggs, beer, in fact many are similar, the main difference being is that most of them are more refined and processed when we get them.) Discuss how the Bandas keep their food as refrigerators are not very common in their country. Draw parallels with Britain in the Victorian or Edwardian times, when food had to be stored, cooked or bottled in order to preserve it.

◆ Organise a class visit to your local supermarket. This can encompass work on transportation of food, jobs linked with the industry, as well as the products sold there. This may have to be booked well in advance as some supermarkets organise very popular visits.

◆ Ask the children to make a list of food they might eat in a day. Then ask them to select one item of food from their list and decide where the food may have come from. Most products are labelled with the country of origin so this can work well as a homework research exercise. Ask them to plot the original country on a world map and the route it has taken to get to the UK, and at the end of the task a really global picture of our food resources should emerge.

Further literacy ideas

◆ In a shared writing lesson, get the children to write out the instructions for making mealie-meal – using bullet points. Remind them to make sure that the tasks are in the right order. Give the children copies of other recipes with the order mixed up and ask them to do the same.

◆ *Obed was looking forward to the next week.* Use this as the basis for the children to write a week of diary entries. Remind them to use the information that they have about the setting for the story and the things they know about Obed's character.

◆ In groups or in pairs, give the children some lyrics from songs sung in countries similar to that described in the story. Ask them to make up some of their own lyrics and set them to a simple tune.

◆ *Suddenly Mrs Banda screamed and stood very still.* Get the children to continue the story from this point, asking them to change the ending to make it different.

◆ Explain to the children that some people might disagree with Mr Banda killing the snake. In a guided writing lesson, discuss the arguments for and against killing the snake. Use this as a starting point for the children to write points of view, for and against particular actions.

Town transect

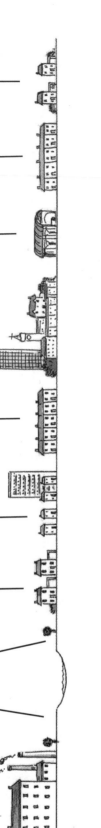

Suburbs and private housing

Old terraced housing

Railway station

Town centre – old buildings, new office blocks and many shops

Old terraced housing

Council estate on site of old houses

Modern private housing estate

Open space either side of river – floodplain and park area

Industrial estate – light manufacturing

Ring road (dual carriageway)

Technology park – high-tech businesses

Genre
diagram with labels

Town transect

Geography learning objectives

◆ To use geographical vocabulary (2a).

◆ To collect, record and analyse evidence (1b, 1c).

◆ To identify how places change (3e).

◆ To compare a place with their own area (3f, 6a).

◆ To carry out fieldwork investigations outside the classroom (7c).

Background notes

Many towns have a similar structure, which is understandable when one considers that they have grown outwards from their old centre. A transect is a cross-section, often shown diagrammatically as in this example, which has annotations as well.

Vocabulary

Transect, ring road, dual carriageway, technology, high-tech, manufacturing, floodplain, private, estate, terraced, suburbs.

Discussing the text

◆ Discuss the title of the text with the children. What do they expect the transect to consist of? What do they think it will look like? Have they come across this word before? (Possibly in maths.) Show the text to the children and ask them again whether or not any of them have come across something like this. Make sure that they understand what the transect shows, and the viewpoint from which it is drawn. Talk about other ways the picture could have been drawn, for example from a bird's-eye view. What would be the advantages of this way of looking at a view? Are there any disadvantages?

◆ Focus on the text accompanying the transect. Do the children think it is necessary? Would it be as effective without the text? Discuss each piece of text with them and discuss terms such as *high-tech*, *technology* and *floodplain*. What sort of businesses would the children expect to find on a technology park? Discuss what would probably be found on the industrial estate. What do the children think that *light manufacturing* means?

◆ Discuss the difference between private and council housing with the class.

◆ Talk about the words *terraced* and *suburbs*. Do the children know what they mean? Can they explain what terraced houses look like?

◆ Who do the children think would find this type of text useful? Explain that they are often used by architects when displaying new ideas, or within museums to show the overall view of an area.

Geography activities

◆ Ask the class: *What is a transect?* What does it show and what does it not show in an area? Where do they think the older, original part of the town is? Why does there appear to be so little building in the areas by the river? (The possibility of flooding or marshy land.) Do they know what a ring road is and why the technology park and the industrial areas are near to it?

◆ Show the children pictures of various types of buildings and ask them to match them up with the features marked on the transect. Enlarge the text and ask the children to cut out or draw pictures of the types of buildings found in each zone. These can be displayed on the wall.

◆ Plan a class visit out to draw a transect of the local area. The children will need to look at a map and identify a suitable route, one which will be easy to navigate along and will show a variety of buildings. This can be done equally successfully across a village, town or suburban area. Before going, discuss with them what they think they are likely to see and how they will record this in the field. They will need to make rough notes outside and transfer these onto a good copy back in the classroom. This activity can be done either individually or in groups.

◆ Discuss the use of transects as a method of sampling land use. Can the children think of anything that is not always recorded? (Other buildings in the area, traffic, the multiple use of buildings.) A small-scale fieldwork project can be carried out to record a number of transects across different directions, which can then be used by the children to fill in a map, creating their own observed landuse of a particular area. The children can practise this activity in and around the school grounds, taking transects across a variety of areas and then filling in a map to show the land use of the school.

◆ Encourage the children to take a series of pictures and draw sketches along the transect walks carried out in the above activities, and also to incorporate items and advertisements from local papers to enhance the quality of their information. Ask them, from memory, to place these in the correct place on the finished transects. They can also be given pictures of places they did not see and predict where these would best fit into the transects.

◆ Using an OS map, the children can draw a line across an area, perhaps the area they walked, in order to either predict the type of land use or to check their findings against the evidence on the map.

◆ Ask the children to draw a transect of a place in one of their reading books. They will need to choose a story which moves through a different environment or is set in a village or town location.

Further literacy ideas

◆ Ask the children to compile a glossary for some of the words in the text. This could be done for a specified audience, for instance it could be written in simple language with illustrations for younger children.

◆ Ask the children to write a newspaper report about a proposed plan to build a development of new houses on the park area shown in the text. Ask the children to choose a point of view to write from, perhaps a young person who would be able to get a job building the houses, or a conservationist who wants to protect the park. Ask the children to write a profile for their character first and to then use this in their writing.

◆ Ask the children to use the text as a basis for writing a description of a place, using full sentences, for example On the outskirts of the town there is a technology park, where there are many high-tech businesses.

◆ Use the word high-tech as a starting point to investigate the use of hyphens and words that are commonly abbreviated with the children, such as information to info.

◆ Get the children to write a story set in the place in the text. They should use some of the features of the town within their story, such as the railway station. Encourage them to plan their story to ensure that it has a beginning, middle and an end.

◆ Use the text to look at compound words with the children, such as floodplain and carriageway. Ask them to find other examples of compound words related to towns.

Town

Bus shelter
Modern bus shelters are usually made of steel and plexiglass and have advertisements on them.

Library
The local library is usually a branch of the county library, so there is a wide range of books to choose from.

Post office
In a large town the post office may also have a sorting office at the back, and a yard for delivery vans.

Town houses
These elegant houses can be found in some towns and cities. They were originally built for rich people as an additional home, when they wanted to visit the town.

Terraced houses
These brick houses can be found in most towns and cities. They were built for workers who moved to the towns in the nineteenth century.

Museum
Many towns have a museum, which tells the history of the area.

Restaurant
Towns are likely to have a wide range of restaurants.

Railway station
Not every town has a railway station. Some stations may be quite small, whilst in large cities there may be a very grand one.

Department store
These large shops have many different sections with a wide variety of goods, such as clothes, food, toys, furniture and cosmetics.

Country

Post bus

In some country areas the bus service is combined with the post service, so people can catch a post bus which goes around delivering post as well.

Cottages

These cottages were built for farm workers about 200 years ago. Other cottages may be older, and some may even have timber (wooden) frames.

Travelling library

Not all people can travel to the large town library, so the travelling library brings a selection of books to the villages.

Bus shelter

People sometimes have to wait for buses in open country in very bad weather, so these shelters have to give good protection.

Farmhouses

Many houses are built on the farms outside villages, but sometimes the farmhouse and the farmyard are in the village itself.

Public house

These are meeting places for people. They are allowed to sell alcohol, but they often serve food and hot drinks as well.

Railway station

Many country stations have been closed and pulled down. Country stations are usually very small, often only a shelter on a platform. If there is no ticket office, a ticket can be bought on the train.

Windfarm

Wind can be used to make electricity. It needs many generators to make enough wind, so they are often grouped together where they will catch the wind more easily.

Village shop

This is where people buy everyday needs if they run out of something. It may also be a post office and sell newspapers. Most people will do their main shopping in a large supermarket.

Town and country

Geography learning objectives
◆ To collect and record evidence (1b).
◆ To use appropriate geographical vocabulary (2a).
◆ To use maps and atlases (2c).
◆ To identify and describe what places are like and to locate them (3a, 3b).

Vocabulary
Post bus, library, travelling, timber, shelter, alcohol, generators, supermarket, plexiglass, elegant, restaurant, museum, department, furniture, cosmetics.

Discussing the text

◆ Put each text, in turn, on an OHP and, covering the captions, show the children some or all of the pictures and ask them to suggest a label or caption for each picture. Make a list of these suggestions on a flip chart and then compare these with the actual text as it is revealed to the children. Have the children heard of, or seen, all of the places identified in the text? Talk about any features that are unfamiliar to them, such as the windfarm. Take a show-of-hands survey for the number of children who have seen each feature and record the results. Discuss the results of this survey with the class.

◆ Read out a few of the features and ask the children to describe what they look like. Tell them to think about how they would describe the feature to someone who had never seen it before.

◆ Read out selected pieces of text and ask the children to guess which feature you are describing.

◆ Give each child a copy of each text and discuss similarities and differences between the two. Can the children explain why there are some features that occur on both lists, such as a bus shelter, and why there are other features that only occur on one list, for instance a museum? Discuss any other features not listed that the children have come across in either a town or the countryside. Are any of the children's suggestions features that could be found in both town and country?

◆ Talk about alternative names that the children can think of for any of the features, for example *café* or *bar* instead of *restaurant*. Why do the children think that there can be more than one name for a place? (Talk about continental influences.)

Geography activities
◆ Decide with the children which of the features can be found in the local area. Does this mean that they live in the town or the country? Discuss the idea of suburban areas – living on the edge of the town or city, as this is a zone that many of the children will live in, or have friends who live there. Ask them to complete a list of features which characterise their own area, in the style of the text.

◆ Use pictures that show features in the local area and discuss with the children the use of symbols to represent these. Look at the OS symbols for various features, including the ones in the local area. Why do they think that such symbols are necessary? How helpful do they find symbols around the place? (Such as for toilets or parking.) Which would be the important symbols to find if they were visiting a town abroad and couldn't speak the language?

◆ Working in pairs get the children to make a list of features that appear on both the town and country pages. Ask them to write a paragraph to explain how and why these features are different.

◆ In pairs, ask the children to record features which appear in only one list. They should explain the function of the feature and state why it is only useful in one of the environments. Then ask the pairs to report back to the class, and discuss the children's ideas.

◆ Explain to the children that symbols are a form of shorthand. What other types of shorthand do they know of? (Morse code, text messaging.) Look at a copy of the Highway Code with the class and discuss the use of symbols in it. What does a symbol *not* tell us about the feature it represents? (Size, age, how many.)

◆ Use a range of OS maps to show the children a series of features linked to a specific type of environment, for example a seaside place, a remote mountain area or a rural landscape. This will help them to recognise that there are different symbols and features in different locations, both town and country. Ask the children to create a walk around a map using symbols as references, for example *We started the walk at (symbol) at grid reference (x, x) and from there we walked south until we came to the (symbol)…* Follow this up by asking them to create a walk around a map for their friends to follow.

Further literacy ideas

◆ Give the children one or more of the captions and ask them to write an explanation of the feature in their own words. Remind them that their descriptions should be brief and to the point, but that their sentences should make sense and have accurate punctuation (capital letters and full stops, and capital letters for any proper nouns).

◆ Ask the children to choose either the town or the country and to produce a leaflet encouraging visitors to come to the place. Talk about the setting out of such a text and model how to write the information about the features in an appropriate style. Point out that they should consider their audience and write using persuasive language.

◆ Prepare a set of comprehension questions based on the text, for example what features usually characterise a country station? Remind the children that their answers need to be written in full sentences and in their own words.

◆ Ask the children to write a story entitled 'Lost in the town' about a character that goes from the country to the town, or vice versa, and gets lost. As preparation, the children could read 'The town mouse and the country mouse'.

◆ Do some work with the children on paragraphs. In a guided writing lesson, model how the different features could be written about in a continuous prose format in separate paragraphs.

◆ Give the children an extract from the text with some deliberate spelling mistakes in it and ask them to write it out correctly. The children could then be given some of the spellings to add to their individual spelling lists.

CHAPTER 4

Environmental geography

The study of environmental geography at Key Stage 2 focuses on the study of an issue, or issues. Although many of these will be of a local nature, they are likely to have implications or links to the wider world.

As with physical and human geography, we are looking at the process of change as it affects the local or world environment. There are many opportunities here to develop aspects of citizenship and the concept of 'stewardship', in terms of our responsibility to others.

A common thread when looking at environmental issues is the concept of 'change', and whether such change is good or not. There is no right or wrong answer to this, because it depends on questions of need, as well as matters of aesthetics (what constitutes a 'beautiful view'?) and values (is a gasometer worth conserving as an artefact of the industrial era?).

Commonly occurring issues concern environmental quality, pollution (which might be chemical, visual or aural), the value or otherwise of conserving something (and the related issue of management – doing nothing is not conserving, in order to conserve we must manage the environment in some way), and reusing, recycling and managing resources.

The texts included in this chapter provide opportunities to discuss the above issues. The related activities also recognise that there are often conflicting opinions about some issues, depending on a person's situation.

Inexpensive progress

Genre
poem

Encase your legs in nylons,
Bestride your hills with pylons
 O age without a soul;
Away with gentle willows
And all the elmy billows
 That through your valleys roll.

Let's say good-bye to hedges
And roads with grassy edges
 And winding country lanes;
Let all things travel faster
Where motor-car is master
 Till only Speed remains.

Destroy the ancient inn-signs
But strew the roads with tin signs
 'Keep Left,' 'M4,' 'Keep Out!'
Command, instruction, warning,
Repetitive adorning
 The rockeried roundabout.

For every raw obscenity
Must have its small 'amenity',
 Its patch of shaven green,
And hoardings look a wonder
In banks of floribunda
 With floodlights in between.

Leave no old village standing
Which could provide a landing
 For aeroplanes to roar,
But spare such cheap defacements
As huts with shattered casements
 Unlived-in since the war.

Let no provincial High Street
Which might be your or my street
 Look as it used to do,
But let the chain stores place here
Their miles of black glass facia
 And traffic thunder through.

And if there is some scenery,
Some unpretentious greenery,
 Surviving anywhere,
It does not need protecting
For soon we'll be erecting
 A Power Station there.

When all our roads are lighted
By concrete monsters sited
 Like gallows overhead,
Bathed in the yellow vomit
Each monster belched from it,
 We'll know that we are dead.

John Betjeman

Inexpensive progress

Geography learning objectives

◆ To observe and record changes in an area (1b, 3e).
◆ To express views about the environment (1d, 4a).
◆ To identify and describe what places are like (3a).
◆ To recognise change in the environment (3e, 5a).

Background notes

This poem takes a very specific stand which provides a good opportunity to get children to disagree strongly with the poet, or more probably, to agree strongly, in which case you can play 'devil's advocate' and put forward the opposing view. In such discussions it is all too easy to have a rosy view of the past, which is not necessarily borne out by the facts.

Vocabulary

Ancient, instruction, repetitive, roundabout, obscenity, amenity, floribunda, aeroplanes, casement, provincial, scenery, concrete.

Discussing the text

◆ Explain to the children that the text is a poem and ask them to predict what it might be about from looking at the title. Ask them to give reasons for their answers.

◆ Read the whole poem through to the children and then ask them to consider it in light of the discussion about the title, and to explain in general terms what point the poet is trying to make. How effective do the children think that John Betjeman is in putting across his point of view? Do they agree with the poet's point of view?

◆ Some of the language in the poem may be unfamiliar to the children. Model how it is sometimes possible to work out the meaning of a particular word by looking at its context (the sentence that the word comes within). Challenge the children to work out the meaning of some of the less well-known words in this way, such as *defacements*, *amenity*.

◆ Discuss the overall rhyming pattern of the poem. Show the children how to record this in the format *AA, B, CC, B*. Do the children think this is a common pattern? Discuss other poetic rhyming patterns that the children have come across.

◆ What expression and intonation does the poem need to get its point of view across? Try reading different verses of the poem aloud with the children, trying to give a different overall 'feeling' to the way it sounds. If the poem were presented in a poetry book, what other illustrations would the children expect to see with it?

◆ Discuss with the children the changes that Betjeman talks about. What sort of world does he talk about in the last verse? Do the children think that this is a real possibility, or do they think he is being too negative and pessimistic? Discuss the possibility that the use of *dead* may not be meant literally. Ask in what other ways can people/the world be seen as dead?

Geography activities

◆ Discuss with the children the changes that Betjeman talks about, for example *strew the roads with tin signs*. Do they think these are necessary? When are signs helpful and when do they become overused? (Signposts and other direction signs are useful, but if there are too many they become confusing. Too many notices can also make a place unattractive.)

◆ What sort of changes have the children noticed in their local area? (The building of new houses or roads, roundabouts or bypasses and new street lighting.) Can they make a list of all the changes? When they have compiled a list they need to have time to reflect and notice, perhaps on their way home, and then add to the list the next day. Why did they not notice the changes in the first place? Ask if they think we become so used to change that we don't notice it's happening.

◆ Look at a copy of the Highway Code signs (also found in many road atlases), and ask the children to notice which categories they fall into – commands, instructions or warnings – as mentioned in the poem. Ask them to draw examples of these signs. How and why are the shapes of the signs different?

◆ Take the class on a walk and have a look in the immediate area of the school for signs. Ask the children to work in pairs and to list them, including those on the road, for example yellow lines. Ask the class, either during the walk or back in the classroom: *Are the signs well positioned? Are they bunched together? If so why?*

◆ Ask the children to take a verse of their choosing from the poem and to draw a picture of how they imagine the landscape to look. Invite them to discuss their choice of features in their pictures.

◆ As a class, contact your local planning office and ask about the process of obtaining planning permission in your area. Ask the children to search in local papers for local planning applications. Why do they think it is important to have planning controls?

◆ In a shared writing lesson, make a note of all the arguments that the poet puts forward against progress, such as the building of motorways. Model with the children how to write counter arguments for some of these points. Then have a class debate, using the poem as a starter, on whether or not change is a good thing in an area. Remember that change can be for the better or for the worse, so an understanding of this should arise from the debate, including the question of 'need' (people need somewhere to live, so houses must be built *somewhere*).

Further literacy ideas

◆ Select a number of words from the poem and ask the children to find definitions for them. Tell them that although they can use dictionaries these meanings must ultimately be written in their own words. This work could be extended so that, in groups, the children provide a glossary for the poem.

◆ Using a selection of poetry books ask the children to find other examples of poems by John Betjeman. They should identify the themes of these poems and write short book-blurb style reviews on the poems, starting with one for 'Inexpensive progress'.

◆ In groups, get the children to compile a report, pulling out the salient points from the poem, and to then assume the roles of a newspaper team. Two children could lay the report out using IT resources, another child could edit the report, someone else compile headings, and so on.

◆ Using a similar theme to that of the poem, ask the children to write a similarly styled poem. Ask them to spend time revising their poem once they've completed it, substituting more evocative words or altering lines, for example, to make it as good as they can.

◆ Get the children to identify the rhyming words in the poem and to make a note of those letter patterns which make the rhyming sound, such as the ee sound in *green* and *between*. Ask the children to find other rhyming words to add to each group by looking for words with the same letter patterns.

Skylines

Genre
illustrations,
and extracts
from classic
fiction and
poetry

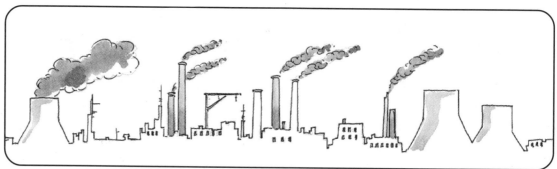

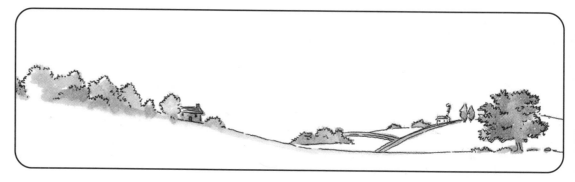

Saturday afternoon in November was approaching the time of twilight, and the vast tract of unenclosed wild known as Egdon Heath embrowned itself moment by moment. Overhead the hollow stretch of whitish cloud shutting out the sky was as a tent which had the whole heath for its floor.

The heaven being spread with this pallid screen and the earth with the darkest vegetation, their meeting-line at the horizon was clearly marked. In such contrast the heath wore the appearance of an instalment of night which had taken up its place before its astronomical hour was come: darkness had to a great extent arrived hereon, while day stood distinct in the sky. Looking upwards, a furze-cutter would have been inclined to continue work; looking down, he would have decided to finish his faggot and go home.

The day is come when I again repose

Here, under this dark sycamore, and view

These plots of cottage-ground, these orchard-tufts,

Which at this season, with their unripe fruits,

Are clad in one green hue, and lose themselves

'Mid groves and copses. Once again I see

These hedge-rows, hardly hedge-rows, little lines

Of sportive wood run wild: these pastoral farms,

Green to the very door; and wreaths of smoke

Sent up, in silence, from among the trees!

A sunny midsummer day. There was such a thing sometimes, even in Coketown.

Seen from a distance in such weather, Coketown lay shrouded in a haze of its own, which appeared impervious to the sun's rays. You only knew the town was there, because you knew there could have been no such sulky blotch upon the prospect without a town. A blur of soot and smoke, now confusedly tending this way, now that way, now aspiring to the vault of Heaven, now murkily creeping along the earth, as the wind rose and fell, or changed its quarter: a dense formless jumble, with sheets of cross light in it, that showed nothing but masses of darkness:- Coketown in the distance was suggestive of itself, though not a brick of it could be seen.

Skylines

Geography learning objectives

◆ To ask geographical questions, analyse evidence and draw conclusions (1a, 1c).

◆ To use appropriate fieldwork techniques (2b).

◆ To identify and describe what places are like (3a).

◆ To explain what places are like and how and why they are changing (3c, 3e).

◆ To recognise environmental issues in the community and how they are changing (6d, 6e).

Vocabulary

Twilight, tract, pallid, vegetation, horizon, distinct, sycamore, orchard, copse, pastoral, midsummer, shrouded, blotch, murkily, impervious.

Discussing the text

◆ Look at the page of skylines with the children. Talk about the angle from which they are drawn. Discuss the words *transect* and *bird's-eye view* and ensure that the children understand these terms.

◆ Discuss some of the skylines with the children. What do they show? Ask the children to give reasons for their assessments, such as differentiating the shape of modern tower blocks compared to factory outlines. Model how to put into words what the skylines show if necessary. Are the children familiar with all the buildings shown in the outlines? Do they know what a power station looks like, for instance?

◆ Look at the third piece of text with the children. Explain that it is taken from a poem by William Wordsworth called 'Lines composed a few miles above Tintern Abbey', which is on the River Wye. Talk about the environment where the poem is written. What clues are there in the poem about the setting (*hedge-rows, pastoral farms*). Discuss the meaning of any unfamiliar words with the children, such as *copse* or *grove*.

◆ Talk about the reference to *wreaths of smoke* in the same poem. Do the children think this reference fits with the description of the area? What does this suggest?

◆ Read the children the fifth piece of written text from *Hard Times* by Charles Dickens and talk with them about Coketown. What sort of place do the children think the author is describing? (Get them to think about the name.) Do the children know of other Dickens texts set in Victorian industrial towns? Does this background knowledge help their understanding of what type of place Coketown is? Refer them back to the Wordsworth poem. Do the children think the phrase *wreaths of smoke* could refer to similar industrial buildings set within the countryside near Tintern Abbey?

Geography activities

◆ Look with the children at the different skylines across the variety of environments. Identify all the details of one in particular with them. Using a magnifying glass may help both identification and concentration. Ask them to identify the features in the other skylines. How much information can be given about a place in this way? Do they think it is a useful way of showing a place?

◆ With the class match the textual descriptions to the skylines. (Answers: Skyline 1 – text 1, *The Return of the Native*; Skyline 2 – text 5, *Hard Times*; Skyline 4 – text 3, 'Lines composed a few miles above Tintern Abbey'.) Discuss with the children what words match up with parts of the skylines.

Then talk about what words they think could be used to describe the two skylines that don't have descriptions. Focus on what sort of environment each skyline is, what sort of atmosphere the place might have, and so on. The children can then try writing a description of each environment. As an additional challenge, they could try to write the descriptions in the style of one of the three already given.

◆ Explain to the children that the three descriptions of skylines are all from the nineteenth century (by Hardy, Wordsworth and Dickens respectively). Discuss with the children how they think these places may have changed (perhaps only slightly in the case of the wilder areas, or maybe there is a motorway running across Egdon Heath now). Do they think that Coketown will have similar industries? Would the pollution be the same? Would the town have grown? What changes would there be in the roads? The children can draw modern skylines for these three places, and then write descriptions to match, or vice versa.

◆ Talk about the local area together and identify the main features. What would these look like in profile? Ask the children to practise first and to then draw a skyline to show the features of their local area. (It may well be that there are several profiles which represent the area.) These could be effectively displayed by placing them on an OS map of the area.

◆ Encourage the children to create other skylines, for example taken from a description in a book they are reading. Some children may be able to look at an OS map in detail and attempt a skyline drawing based on that.

◆ Drawing a skyline is a good introduction for children to the concept of land use – the notion that types or categories of land use in any area can be identified and therefore mapped. Using a map of your area, take the children out to try and identify the major land uses around them. Get them to select colours to represent different uses, such as housing, industrial, recreational, transport links, and back in the classroom ask them to make a fair copy. It may be necessary to select the principal use of an area, as it will be unlikely that each area will have a sole use. Discuss these issues with the children.

◆ Ask the children to read the description about Coketown carefully. What are the characteristics that identify it as an industrial town? Get them to think about industries in the UK today or perhaps those in the area around you. What are the characteristics of these in the modern world? Get the children to make a list of modern industrial features on the left-hand side of a sheet of paper, such as buildings, power resources, workers, and industrial features in Victorian times. Can they think why there are such differences between the two periods of history? (Tell them about the Great Smog of 1952 which led to the Clean Air Act of 1956.)

Further literacy ideas

◆ Ask the children to rewrite the Egdon Heath passage in modern-day language.

◆ Give the class examples of other poems written by William Wordsworth. Ask them to learn some of these, such as 'Daffodils' and to perform them in groups.

◆ Ask the children to bring in, or choose from the library, a poem and to write a review of it, stating why they chose it.

◆ Get the children to write a rhyming poem about one of the landscapes described.

◆ The children could make a list of the words from the texts that are not in common usage today, such as *furze*. They could make a second list of words that we use instead.

◆ Investigate homographs with the children based on words in the text, such as *faggot – a meatball* or *a bundle of sticks bound together as fuel.*

Climber's tip top mission

Luke Harding in Katmandu

© Oxford Scientific/www.osf.uk.com

It is a huge task, removing the rubbish left behind by hundreds of expeditions up the world's highest mountain.

When the Japanese climber Ken Noguchi set off last year to clean up the Tibetan side of Mount Everest he was startled by some of the things he and his team found – not just discarded oxygen cylinders and tents but empty beer bottles, rusting tin cans and empty noodle packets.

Setting off for the Tibetan capital, Lhasa, on his second clean-up mission with a team of 40 drawn from five countries, Noguchi, 27, said he had decided to remover the rubbish on Everest after his first visit in 1997, when he was appalled by the amount of junk.

"I was so angry," he said. "I had always assumed that Everest was in pristine condition. In fact it is very dirty."

Since Edmund Hilary and Tenzing Norgay conquered Everest in 1953, 572 expeditions have tried to reach the summit. Over the years the rubbish they have left behind has grown to the point where the mountain has been called the world's highest rubbish tip.

Environmentalists estimate that, despite the recent attempts to remove some of it, 100 tonnes of waste lie on its slopes.

Five years ago the Nepalese government introduced a £2800 bond payable by those wanting to climb the steep glacial southern route – as well as the £49 000 permit fee – refundable only when teams brought their junk down.

As a result the Nepalese side became much cleaner. No such scheme exists on the longer northern approach in Tibet, which is controlled by the Chinese authorities.

"The Tibet side is full of garbage," Noguchi said. "One of the problems is human excrement. People just use the grass. There is no bacteria at this altitude, so nothing decomposes. Lower down the valley people drink water from the glacier."

"It was a big shock to find so many things from Japan," he added. "But then Everest is merely a reflection of human society, so we should not be surprised at the debris left behind."

Text © *The Guardian*, 12 April 2001

The Everest Years

Genre
autobiography

And then suddenly I was there. Odd, Bjorn and Pertemba were beckoning to me, shouting, their voices muffled by their oxygen masks. I crouched in a foetal position and just cried and cried in great gasping sobs – tears of exhaustion, tears of sorrow for so many friends, and yet tears of fulfilment for something I had so much needed to do and had done with people who had come to mean a great deal to me. I had at last reached the summit of Everest.

I suspect that every climber in the world dreams of standing on the highest point on earth; certainly every climber who joins an expedition to Everest does and that includes quite a few of the Sherpa high-altitude porters as well. If you judge success, therefore, in terms of the sum of individual satisfaction and fulfilment, there is a very real point in getting as many to the summit as possible. Getting there quickly both increases the chance of success and reduces the time that the team is exposed to danger.

There were five expeditions attempting Everest by different routes in the spring of 1985 and the speed with which we were able to run out the route undoubtedly contributed to the fact that we were the only successful expedition. The others were overtaken by the bad weather that occurred later in the season. We were fast because we had a superb and very strong Sherpa force and because the climbers and Sherpas became welded into a closely knit team who worked happily, and therefore effectively, together.

It was this that made the expedition such a success, not just in terms of making records, but also in terms of personal satisfaction for every member of the team. I have been on expeditions that have reached their summit and yet there has been little sense of success because the group had failed to work together and there was acrimony rather than friendship at the end of the experience.

Unless you always go alone, the essence of climbing is teamwork. You are entrusting your life to others, on a rock climb to your partner holding the other end of the rope, but on a higher mountain it becomes more complex. There you need to trust the judgement of others in choosing a route, or perhaps their ability to give support from a lower camp. There is a constant interplay of decision-making, be it between two climbers on a crag in the Lake District or amongst thirty distributed between a series of camps on Everest.

Chris Bonnington

Everest

Geography learning objectives

◆ To ask geographical questions (1a).

◆ To analyse evidence and draw conclusions (1c).

◆ To use atlases and globes to locate places (2c, 3b).

◆ To use ICT to help in geographical investigations (2f).

◆ To recognise how people affect the environment and understand the need for sustainable development (5a, 5b).

Background notes

These texts provide a rich source of information on Mount Everest and the nature of exploration. The texts themselves, and the work the children are asked to do, are challenging materials and will provide excellent extension work for more able pupils.

Vocabulary

Expedition, Tibet, oxygen cylinder, summit, Everest, glacial, treacherous, mountaineering, exhaustion, Sherpa, experience.

Discussing the text

◆ Show the children the newspaper article 'Climber's tip top mission'. Can they identify the type of text it is by looking at its layout?

◆ Do the children know where Katmandu is? Read the first paragraph (in bold) of the text with them. Do they know what the world's highest mountain is called?

◆ After reading through the article, ask the children if they are surprised by the story. Have they ever considered that explorers are polluting mountainous areas?

◆ Discuss the £2800 bond. What is this? Why do the children think that the Nepalese government introduced this? If the intention was to reduce the number of people visiting the mountain do the children think this will work, and if not why not?

◆ Talk about the reference to the Tibet side. Do the children know why the mountain is controlled by two governments (discuss its location)?

◆ Address the final sentence of the article, *But then Everest is merely a reflection of human society, so we should not be surprised at the debris left behind.* What do the children think the first part of the sentence means? Why might some readers be offended by the whole comment? (Discuss this in terms of opinion and fact.)

◆ Read the text entitled 'The Everest Years' with the class and discuss how its writing style (autobiography) differs from the newspaper article.

◆ Discuss the personal satisfaction that the author refers to in the text. What do the children think would drive someone to want to climb Mount Everest? Do any of them feel a similar drive?

◆ Ask the children if they know who the Sherpas are? Where do they come from? How are they involved in the Mount Everest expeditions and why are they so important?

◆ Discuss why the children think the author refers to some expeditions as having not been as successful, even though the climbers reached the summit of Everest.

Geography activities

◆ Use a range of pictures of the Everest area to bring the scenery alive for the children. These are available on the Internet (get the children to search for Mount Everest) or in library books. Talk about the environment in which the mountain lies. Use an atlas to locate the Himalayas and in particular the mountains, ridges and towns of the area. Look with them at the changes in the climatic and vegetation maps of the area and talk to the children about the lower reaches of the mountain in comparison with the snowy tops.

◆ Look at the area in a world setting with the children. Which countries are close to Mount Everest? Which govern the way in which it is used? Where is Europe and the UK in relation to the mountain? Can they work out the distance to travel there? Get the children to mark the main places on a map and label them.

◆ Discuss the environmental problem which is developing on Mount Everest. Ask the children: *What sort of litter is collecting there? Why do people leave it there? Why don't they bury it? Why does the litter not decompose?* Ask the children to design posters to place at strategic points around the base of the mountain to encourage people to take a more responsible attitude to dealing with their litter.

◆ Ask the children to carry out some research on Mount Everest and its importance to the countries in the area. Information can be accessed via the Internet. Sites such as www.everestnews.com and www.cbc.ca/everest2000 will provide a range of resources, such as diaries of trekking, pictures and facts and figures about the area. This information could be used as the basis for a class display on the world's highest mountain.

◆ Mount Everest, like Antarctica and the North polar regions, is a great wilderness place. Develop a debate with the children as to whether or not these places should be visited and if so, should tourists be limited and how could governments go about doing this?

Further literacy ideas

◆ Ask the children to imagine they are interviewing one of the Everest climbers. What questions would they like to ask? Get them to write their questions in a list, in the order in which they want to ask them. Can they predict some of the answers to the questions?

◆ Extract a list of difficult words from the texts, and give the children a selection of dictionaries to help them find the definitions. They should compare the definitions from the various dictionaries.

◆ Challenge the children to write some alternative headlines for the newspaper article.

◆ Talk to the children about biographies. Ask them to research the life of an explorer or mountaineer and to write an article about them.

◆ Tell the children to imagine they have just reached the summit of Everest. Ask them to write a letter home explaining their achievement and how they feel about this.

◆ Get the children to use non-fictional reference books to research the politics of Everest – the Nepalese and the Chinese sides. They can add this information to the display made in the geography activity, above.

Genre
newspaper
article

All rise:

Venetians are losing that sinking feeling

John Follain

Rising damp: St Mark's Square floods regularly yet has risen by a centimetre in 25 years

Photo © Agence France-Presse/Andrea Merola

Venice may still be in peril. However, the city known as La Serenissima is no longer sinking, but rising.

A new study from experts appointed by the Italian environment ministry has discovered that the level of the ground surrounding St Mark's Square – among the lowest-lying in Venice – has been raised by half a centimetre since 1973. Several other parts of the city's historic centre are as much as one centimetre higher.

Scientists say the city has been rising since a halt was called to the pumping of large amounts of ground water from artesian wells running under the city. The water supplied an industrial complex at Marghera on the mainland nearby.

This had dried out the rock below and allowed Venice to sink by up to 12cm. Since the water has begun flowing back in, the rock has swollen like a sponge, pushing up the level of the alleyways and buildings.

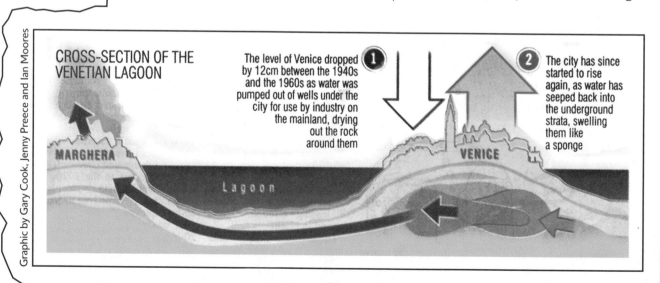

Graphic by Gary Cook, Jenny Preece and Ian Moores

CROSS-SECTION OF THE VENETIAN LAGOON

① The level of Venice dropped by 12cm between the 1940s and the 1960s as water was pumped out of wells under the city for use by industry on the mainland, drying out the rock around them

② The city has since started to rise again, as water has seeped back into the underground strata, swelling them like a sponge

MARGHERA

VENICE

Lagoon

© Times Newspapers, 17 January 1999

All rise

Geography learning objectives
◆ To ask questions, analyse evidence and draw conclusions (1a, 1c).
◆ To identify and explain different viewpoints about topical geographical issues (1d).
◆ To locate, identify and describe what a place is like (3a, 3b, 3c).
◆ To recognise physical and human processes (4b).
◆ To recognise how people can improve and manage the environment (5a, 5b).

Background notes
This article on the flood problems in Venice brings together a major environmental issue which faces many countries and a famous Italian city, which is more stereotypically well known for its images of canals, gondolas, ice creams and long hot summers. This provides the opportunity for children to learn about the difference between the image of a place and the reality.

Vocabulary
Venice, industry, underground, strata, environment, flood, low-lying, artesian wells.

Discussing the text
◆ Focus on the headline *All rise: Venetians are losing that sinking feeling.* What do the children predict the text might be about? Ask them to focus on the photograph with the caption *Rising damp* as a clue.
◆ Do the children know what part of the world Venetians come from? Ask if they know anything about the city of Venice. Read the first paragraph of the article with them, explaining that La Serenissima is the poetic name used for Venice, and then discuss with the children the uniqueness of Venice and its location.
◆ Read through the whole article with the children and it. Ask them questions to assess their understanding of what is happening to Venice. Do the children feel that the explanation is clear? Can they suggest a way of making the text clearer? (Perhaps by using simpler language.) Look at the labelled diagram of Venice with the children. Do the children think the diagram is a useful addition to the article and does it aid their understanding of the text?

Geography activities
◆ Discuss with the children the location of Venice. Ask them where they think it is and then use atlases and maps to locate Europe, Italy and Venice. Ask them to write about or describe the location of the city using the maps for reference. If they were going to visit Venice, how could they travel and which route would they take?
◆ Find out from the children what they know about Italy. What sort of picture emerges from their contributions? Are they then surprised to see the article on Venice which talks of rainfall, flooding and problems more usually associated with northern European places? This is a good opportunity to show some brochure pictures of the holiday atmosphere of Italy and discuss the image versus the reality dichotomy which will exist in any country.

◆ Discuss why the problem of flooding is happening in Venice and why it has taken so long to do anything about it. Tell the children they have been asked to write a short account of what is happening for their local paper. They will need to work out the main points, such as *What is the problem? Where is it happening? Why is it happening? How can it be resolved?* They will need to design and write their newspaper article, and chose a suitable headline. Make a display of their finished work.

◆ Ask the children to investigate why Venice is such an important tourist city. What are the main features? Why do people go there? Why are the canals so important? Give groups of children different aspects to research and present their findings to the class. A good way of researching information is to type in 'Venice Italy' into an Internet search engine and a number of sites of interest can be found (www.freefoto.com/pictures/italy/venice is a site that has some excellent pictures of the main sites in Venice).

◆ Relate the flooding problems to those which occur in the UK. Nearly every year there are some major floods here and these have a big impact on housing, people, farming or other local businesses and transport links. Show pictures of flooded areas and if possible some video footage, such as a main news item from the TV. Discuss with the children the effects of flooding, for example, on where they live. If their house were to be threatened how would they cope? (Move furniture upstairs, buy in food.) Would the problem still be there if they lived in a flat which is higher above the floodwaters?

◆ Ask the children to find out from a dictionary or encyclopaedia what an artesian well is. Then ask them to draw a diagram to show how they are formed and to write a short explanation of what they are and how they work.

Further literacy ideas

◆ Give the children a list of words from the text and ask them to find their meanings using a dictionary. It may be necessary to provide the children with a geographical dictionary.

◆ Use the caption *Rising damp* from the photograph as a story title for the class. Get them to set their story in the city of Venice and include some of the detail from the article, such as St Mark's Square or La Serenissima.

◆ Give the children a selection of newspaper headlines and ask them to predict what the articles are about. Compare the children's suggestions with the actual articles.

◆ In a shared writing lesson, identify the main features of newspaper articles of this type – the tense, the use of technical language, the inclusion of comments from interested parties. Model how to write such an article for the children. Then ask them to write a short newspaper article about Venice. Encourage them to use reference books and the Internet to research their articles, explaining that this is what journalists do.

◆ Ask the children to choose one of the characters in the photograph and to write a profile for them. They can then write a story that includes one or more of these characters.

Survey on pollution

Genre questionnaire

We are doing some research on views about pollution. Please answer *yes* or *no* to the following questions:

1. Do you think air quality is an important issue today?

2. Do you think we have too many cars on the road?

3. Do you often find parking a problem?

4. Do you think cars pollute the environment?

5. Is air pollution a problem in towns today?

6. Do you think more people should use public transport to get around?

7. Do you think traffic should be limited or banned in some cities?

8. Do you think car pollution affects people's health?

SO, would YOU be prepared to give up YOUR car?

Survey on pollution

Geography learning objectives

◆ To ask geographical questions (1a).

◆ To collect, record and analyse evidence (1b, 1c).

◆ To use appropriate fieldwork techniques and ICT in geographical investigations (2b, 2f).

◆ To identify how and why places change (3e).

◆ To recognise that people can improve or damage the environment and see the processes involved (4b, 5a, 5b).

Vocabulary

Survey, pollution, research, questions, quality, issue, environment, problem, limited, health, prepared.

Discussing the text

◆ Start by discussing the title with the children and ask if they know what a survey is. Have they ever conducted a survey before? If so, what was it about? How did they collect the results and what did they do with them?

◆ Tell the children that the survey in the text consists of a series of questions. Can they suggest what the questions might be about? Record some of the children's suggestions and compare these with the actual text.

◆ Discuss the phrase *air quality* that is used in the first question. Do the children understand what it means? Can they think of an alternative way of asking the question?

◆ Ask the children to answer the questions in the text and to give a show of hands for their answers. Ask them to suggest how you could record the results and do this on a flip chart. Can they suggest how to record an answer where someone says that they're not sure about a question, or doesn't answer a straightforward *yes* or *no?*

◆ Ask the children to consider the question at the end of the survey. Why do they think this is written in bold? What do the children think most people's answer to this question would be? Encourage the children to give reasons for their answers.

Geography activities

◆ Discuss with the children the best way of conducting a survey to sample viewpoints. Review the effectiveness of those questions which only require a *yes* or *no* answer. Compare them to questions which ask *where*, *what*, *why* and *how*. Which type of questions do they think are more likely to give really helpful information? On reflection, ask them if the questionnaire in the text is a 'real' one or a 'trick' one? (That is, one which traps you into the punchline at the end.)

◆ Ask the children to rewrite the questions so that real viewpoints can be collected. So question 1 might be *How important do you think air quality is as an issue today?* This could have three boxes to tick for different levels of response – very important, fairly important, of little importance. Discuss how the provision of boxes helps to make the collation of data easier.

◆ Suggest to the children that they may like to carry out the survey and use the information from

the completed questionnaire. If everyone in the class completes two or three of them at home, or over a weekend, this will provide a significant amount of easily collected data which can be entered on a simple spread sheet for analysis. When the results are ready these can be discussed and the children asked to write a short report on their findings.

◆ Identify a particular issue in your area and ask the class to draw up an appropriate questionnaire to investigate it. They will need to review what they know about questionnaires and their construction, before embarking on a project such as this.

◆ Ask the children to fill in a weekly timetable recording when their family car is used (if they have one). Make a class list of the ways in which cars are used and then indicate the alternatives each family member could use for a week instead. The children could share this at home if they have a car and see what their family feels about the plan.

◆ Ask the children to suggest ways of reducing the use of the car. These might include car-sharing, using the bus or walking. Find out about how other countries reduce the number of cars on their roads. For example, in America car-sharing is promoted and more than two people in a car ensures that that car is allowed onto the freeway immediately in the rush hour and can travel in a special lane.

Further literacy ideas

◆ Revise the use of question marks with the class. Give the children a series of sentences and questions, with no question marks. Ask them to identify those which require a question mark.

◆ Ask the children to answer the questions in the text in full written sentences. They could do this work with a partner, writing down the answers they give.

◆ Many of the questions in the survey start with the word *Do*. Ask the children to brainstorm a list of question words, such as *what*, *which*, *how*, and ask them to experiment with changing the first word in each question. Do the questions still make sense? How could they make them make sense again?

◆ Consider the last question on the survey in bold with the children. Ask them to invent their own slogans that will encourage people to stop and think about pollution. They could write a simple playscript for a sketch that demonstrates what ordinary people can do to stop pollution.

◆ Use some of the words in the text, such as *environment*, *pollution* and *important*, to revise spelling strategies, such as the breaking down of words into phonemes in order to learn how to spell them.

PHOTOCOPIABLE

Genre
text that raises an issue (a factual note that accompanies a piece of fiction writing)

The house that moved

— Author's note —

The house that moved is a real house that stands at the bottom of West Street in Exeter. Next door to it is a ladies' hairdressing salon the owners of which are friends of mine called Barry Webb and Barry Casley. In 1962 when most of the old West Quarter of the city was being pulled down to make way for the construction of the Inner Bypass, many people thought that the Tudor house on the corner of Frog Street and Edmund Street should be preserved, although it stood directly in the line of the proposed new road. The City Council agreed, and so it was transported three hundred yards to its present site, using the machinery and methods I have described, though the whole operation took much longer than I have suggested. The house has no particular historical significance, but it is a beautiful example of the architecture of the early sixteenth century. It is now used as a jeweller's shop.

The Teignmouth Inn was demolished in exactly the way as it is in the story, but the loss of the West Quarter was not all a tale of sad destruction. Over the centuries the river had shifted its course and left the ancient Exe Bridge high and dry; houses were built over it, but, when they were pulled down, the eastern half of the bridge was revealed once more, battered, but on the whole marvellously intact. Together with the ruins of St Edmund's church it is an impressive monument, the longest medieval bridge left in England. You can walk on it and underneath it, and explore the remains of building even older than the Tudor house itself.

David Rees

The house that moved

Geography learning objectives

◆ To collect, record and analyse evidence (1b, 1c).

◆ To use appropriate fieldwork techniques and ICT in geographical investigations (2b, 2f).

◆ To describe where places are and what they are like (3a–d).

◆ To recognise and explain patterns in housing (4a).

◆ To recognise how people can improve the environment (5a, 5b).

Background notes

This might be an appropriate extract to use if the class has been studying an aspect of history such as the Tudors or the Victorians, or has been looking at settlements in geography.

Vocabulary

Author, hairdressing, quarter, bypass, Tudor, machinery, methods, significance, architecture, jeweller, centuries, impressive, monument, medieval, bridge.

Discussing the text

◆ Show the children the title of the text and discuss with them what an 'Author's note' might be. Have they come across this phrase before and if so, in what context? Was it at the beginning or the end of a story and what did it consist of? Ask them what the purpose of such information is. Why do they think the author writes such a note rather than including the information in the main text of the story?

◆ Read through the text with the children. From the information given can they suggest what the main plot of the story might be?

◆ Discuss this text in terms of fiction or non-fiction. What would the children class this text as? Point out that it tells us that the story which precedes it is based on fact, so it is a non-fiction piece of text.

◆ The author suggests that some things in the story did not actually happen as described. Discuss with the children the concept of 'poetic licence', when an author adds details or events to a piece of fiction that are only partially true. Can the children think of other stories where they know that the author has based a story on a true story but made some alterations? Suggest legends, such as Robin Hood or Arthur and the sword Excalibur. Why do the children think that writers add their own ideas and changes to stories?

Geography activities

◆ Discuss with the children how towns and cities grow up, that each one has a historical background over centuries. How might we find evidence of the past in a town? (Street names, old buildings, maps, museums, or even by word of mouth.) Do they know any background to the local area? What sort of evidence is available to give them clues? Make a class list entitled 'What we know about how our local area has developed' and include things that the children would like to find out. Ask them to suggest how and where they might be able to find the answers, then conduct research as a class.

◆ Ask the children to find a map of Exeter (www.multimap.com is a good source) and to see how much of the information in the extract they can trace. What are some of the other features they can find in Exeter? What is the name of the river, for example, and what is its course like? Where does it enter the sea?

◆ Ask the children to use a road map or atlas to help them work out distance and routes to Exeter from the school. This can be extended into a game or quiz, for example *If you travel 200 miles north from school which main city will you arrive at?* More complex routes can be added for more able children.

◆ Use a variety of pictures of buildings from different periods of history, such as Georgian, Victorian or Tudor, which show typical features of that time. Talk about these features and ask the children to make a list of what they might expect to see in buildings of particular historical periods. Then ask them to work out what they think characterises modern houses and to make a list of these features.

◆ The text talks of a *proposed new road*. Why do the children think this might have been necessary? (To ease traffic congestion.) What happens today in town centres, particularly where there are small, narrow streets? How can congestion in towns be helped by other means than building a bypass? (One-way streets, pedestrian walkways, controlled parking zones.)

Further literacy ideas

◆ Ask the children to write a story entitled 'The house that moved'. Encourage them to write a story plan first, outlining what is going to happen in their story and when. This activity could be modelled in a shared session on how to plan a story and how to build scenes that lead up to a main point of action.

◆ Ask the children to imagine that they are one of the people who think the house should be preserved and object to the building of the Inner Bypass. Get them to write a letter to the local newspaper or the county council stating their objections clearly. As an extension activity they could try and draft possible replies from the paper or authority.

◆ The house would have seen many occupants come and go over the years. The children could write a story from the point of view of the house, making comments about some of the people who have lived there, how it felt about them, which people it was sad to see go and which it was glad to be rid of.

◆ Ask the children to write a newspaper article with the headline 'Transporting the house', about the house being moved. Ask them to imagine they are on-the-scene reporters, and to record the event. They should describe what happens and what they see and feel, such as the gasps of the crowd as the final pieces are put into place.

◆ Ask the children to use non-fiction reference books to find out more information about archaeological digs, and how often conservationists go to great lengths to save buildings and their contents. In small groups, get them to make a short presentation entitled 'Why we need to look after our past'. Discuss the meaning of this title before they start.

◆ Revise the use of capital letters for proper nouns with the class. Identify together the proper nouns in the text, or give the children a passage with some of the proper nouns left out and ask them to write them in correctly.

Geographical skills

This chapter contains a selection of texts that are related to geography in a variety of ways but which do not really fit into any of the geographical classifications of the preceding chapters. Some of the texts can be used to hone children's specific geographical skills, such as using an atlas or geographical dictionary, while others pick up on the skills of using textual and/or tabulated information to gather geographical information.

The 'Read this, or get lost' text contains a variety of textual styles and, when looked at as a whole, forms an interesting piece of persuasive writing. The inclusion of timetables and their accompanying notes, whether embedded in other texts or, as in the case of the Settle–Carlisle timetable, as an independent text, are useful to enable children to find out how well-connected different places are (think how different the bus timetables would be for a medium-sized town and a small village). 'Make a visitor's guide' is a generic text which can be used towards the end of many geography study units as one form of assessment activity. It will give an indication of what children have learned and understood about the place they have been studying.

Colours in our landscape

*Genre
non-fiction,
information
text*

The sky

Why is the sky blue?

If we were standing on the
moon we would see the sun as white and the
sky as black since there is no atmosphere to
scatter the light. When sunlight enters the
earth's atmosphere tiny gas particles –
molecules of oxygen and nitrogen – scatter the
light, particularly the blue wavelengths, so the
sky appears blue and the sun appears yellow.

What are clouds?

Clouds are collections of water droplets. Their
colour depends on how thick they are. Thick
heavy storm clouds do not allow much light
through so they appear grey or black. Sunlight
may reflect off them making them coloured –
for example evening clouds may be tinged
pink by the setting sun.

Why do we see the moon?

The moon reflects sunlight so we can see it – it
does not produce light like the sun does.

Why does the sun appear red at sunrise and sunset?

At sunrise and sunset the sun is low on the
horizon and its light has further to travel
through the atmosphere to reach our eyes, so
more of the wavelengths have been scattered.
Only those at the red end of the spectrum
reach our eyes so the sun appears red.

"Red sky at night shepherd's delight, red sky in the morning fisherman's warning" – is this true?

In Britain, rain usually comes in from the west,
so if the rising sun is reflecting off clouds in the
west making the morning sky red it usually
means that rain is on the way. If clouds in the
west are breaking up and clear skies are on
their way, the red setting sun will be visible
through them and reflected off them making
the evening sky red.

Why do objects a long way off look paler than those which are closer?

Light reflected from these objects has to travel
a long way to our eyes and much of it is
scattered by dust and other particles, such as
water vapour, in the air. The greater the
distance the less light reaches our eyes and
the paler the object appears.

What is a rainbow?

When sunlight passes through raindrops they
act like tiny prisms. The sunlight is split into its
different wavelengths so we see all the colours
of the rainbow.

What are shadows?

When light hits a solid
object and cannot pass
through it, it casts a
shadow on the ground –
more light is passing either
side of it and hitting the ground, so the ground
behind the object looks darker.

Other colours in the landscape

Is soil always brown?

No! The colour of soil depends largely on the
minerals which have been added to it from the
rocks underneath. For example, in parts of
Devon, red sandstone contains large amounts
of iron oxide which makes the soils reddish.
The grey-white soils found on the North and
South Downs contain large amounts of white
calcium carbonate from the chalk underneath.

Why are buildings different colours?

The colours of buildings
depend on the rocks or man-
made materials from which
they are built and on whether
they are covered in some sort of special paint.
Buildings – especially older ones – are often
made from the rock or other deposits found in
the area, because it is cheapest to build with
local materials. For example, in north Wales,
most roofs are made from the local grey slate.
In the south-east of England deposits of clay are
good for making red tiles and bricks.

Why isn't water always blue?

Clean clear water appears blue
because, like gas molecules in the
air, water molecules scatter the
blue light more than wavelengths
at the other end of the spectrum.
Water, however, often contains larger particles
such as microscopic living organisms, mud,
peat or other sediments. These absorb or reflect
various wavelengths so the water appears in
shades of green, yellow or brown depending
on which wavelengths reach our eyes.

Colours in our landscape

Geography learning objectives

◆ To ask geographical questions, collect and record evidence (1a, 1b).

◆ To use a variety of sources of information and fieldwork techniques (2b, 2d).

◆ To recognise and explain patterns (4a).

Vocabulary

Landscape, atmosphere, particles, molecules, wavelength, horizon, spectrum, shepherd, vapour, prism, minerals, rainbow.

Discussing the text

◆ Tell the children the title of the text. What do they predict it will be about? Do they think that it will be a fiction or a non-fiction text?

◆ Explain that the next sub-heading in this text is 'The sky' and that it starts with the question, *Why is the sky blue?* Ask the children to suggest other questions that could be asked about the sky, or about information they would like to know, such as *What is it made of? Why does it have clouds?*

◆ Give each child a copy of the text. read together the answer to the first question and discuss it. Do the children think that it is clear? Is there any vocabulary used that they think needs explaining, such as *wavelengths.* Talk about how the technical vocabulary in a text could be explained, for example with a glossary of terms.

◆ Look at the other questions asked about the sky. Are the children surprised by any of those chosen by the author? Would they replace any of the questions with suggestions from their own list? Ask them to give reasons for their suggestions.

◆ Talk about the saying *Red sky at night shepherds delight…* Have the children heard this before? Do they know of any other weather sayings, such as *It's raining cats and dogs.*

◆ Consider the second part of the text entitled *Other colours in the landscape.* Are there any questions about this subject not posed by the author that the children would like to know the answer to. Make a list of these questions on a flip chart to research at a later date.

Geography activities

◆ Ask the children to write down their own answers to some of the questions in the text. Discuss how difficult they found this exercise. Is it because we take things for granted or that we are not usually asked to explain such everyday things? Can they think of questions they can ask about other aspects of the environment, such as why are some clouds grey or tinged with black? Record these on the flip chart and ask them to then write down explanations, to review them with a partner, choose the best answer and report back to the class.

◆ Working in small groups, get the children to list all the landscape features mentioned in the text. Ask them to draw a large picture of a landscape and mark on as many of the features as they can, labelling them correctly. This can also be created as a collage on the classroom wall, and the children asked to make up some of their own questions about colour in the landscape, attaching them to the collage.

◆ Look at a range of colour pictures of different landscapes with the children and identify the variety of colourful images in each one. Are there are surprising colours? Is there a difference between real colours and artistic impressions? How many different grades or shades of colour can they see? Photocopy one or two of the pictures in black and white, and then ask the children to compare the original with the black and white copy. What qualities does colour bring to the pictures?

◆ Collect samples of materials from the school grounds or places near the school, for example soil or vegetation. Ask the children to identify the principal colours. What makes the basic colours change? Get them to use a dictionary to find out what *humus* and *bedrock* mean. What effect do they have on the colour of soil? Ask also what effect shade or full sunlight has on the colour of vegetation. The children can record examples of these at home and bring in their findings for a class discussion.

◆ Discuss with the children the subtle changes of colour which they may come across in their environment. For example, the colour of clouds. Ask the class to organise a cloud check every half hour or hour throughout the day. They can design a chart and record cloud type (layer clouds, or 'stratus'; heap clouds, or 'cumulus'; and wispy feather clouds, or 'cirrus'), amount of cloud cover and colours observed. Discuss the variations they have noticed and make a display or report of their findings. This sort of exercise is particularly effective on a day which has rainy showers interspersed with sunny intervals, or in winter when darkness comes early.

Further literacy ideas

◆ Use the text as a starting point for looking at the use of parenthetic dashes in writing. Ask the children to find examples of these in their own reading books or in non-fiction reference books. Set the children an exercise, which requires them to put dashes in the correct place.

◆ Investigate weather sayings, such as the one quoted in the text. Follow this work by looking at idioms, such as *Turning over a new leaf*. Working in pairs, ask the children to draw pictures to show what these phrases actually mean and to write explanations for them.

◆ Ask the children to write a story set in the countryside entitled 'Camouflage' about the colours in the landscape camouflaging someone or something. They should compile a story plan before starting the actual story.

◆ Ask the children to choose a similar theme as that in the text, such as colour in nature, research it and then present their ideas in a similar format to that of the text. Draw their attention to the question-and-answer format, writing in paragraphs, and using headings and question marks.

◆ Ask the children to compile a glossary to accompany the text, listing words such as *spectrum*, *molecules*, *sediment*. You may want to refer them to a glossary, and talk about what it is and how it is arranged before they start this exercise.

◆ Use the text to compile a list of proper nouns, common nouns and, if the children are ready for it, abstract nouns. Record these words on a flip chart under the correct category of noun.

PARAGON HOTEL

BIRMINGHAM

Genre
information
text and map

Paragon Hotel
Alcester Street, Birmingham B12 0PJ

Tel: 0121 627 0627   Fax: 0121 627 0628
www.paragonhotel.co.uk

Public Transport

 By Rail, Birmingham New Street Station
Upon leaving the train, head towards the "B" end of the platform. Follow signs for "Way out/Victoria Square".
Taxis are available from the station.

 By Bus
Please contact the Centro Hotline on 0121 200 2700 or your local operator for information and timetables.

 By Air, Birmingham International Airport
Situated at junction 6 of the M42 (see locator map below). Journey time approximately 15-30 minutes drive to the city centre.

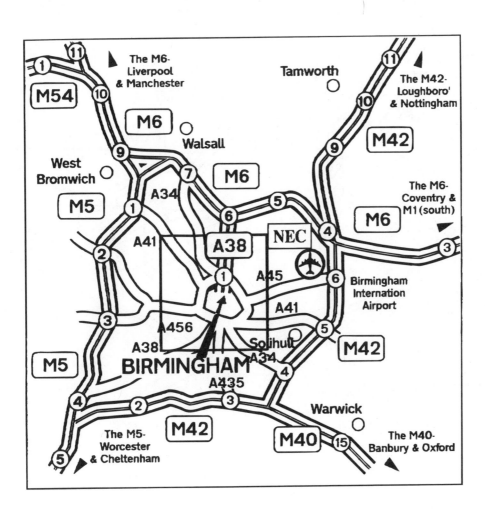

PARAGON HOTEL

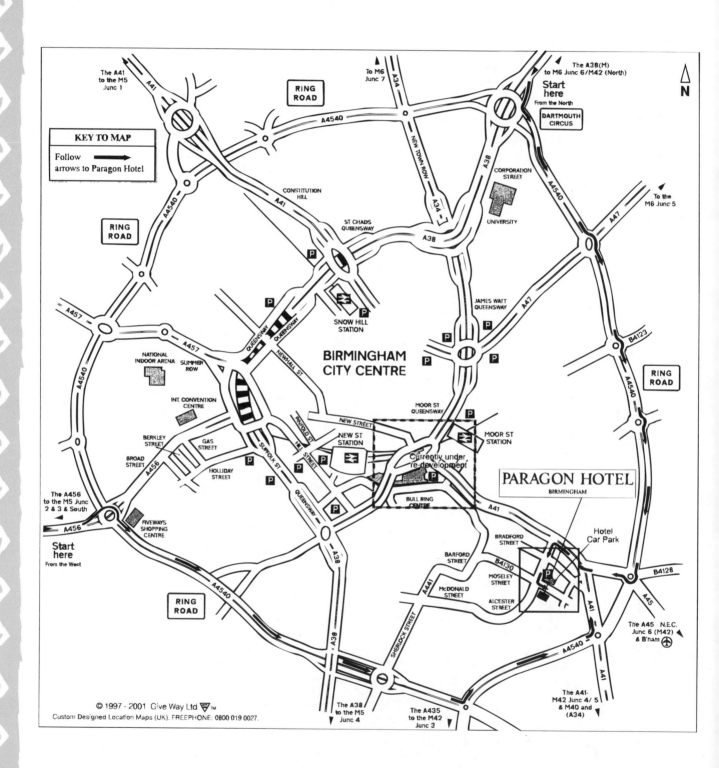

Paragon hotel

Geography learning objectives

◆ To ask geographical questions and use appropriate geographical vocabulary (1a, 2a).

◆ To use appropriate secondary resources, maps and atlases (2c, 2d).

◆ To describe where places are and how to get there (3b, 3c).

◆ To recognise how places fit within a wider geographical context (3g).

◆ To learn about a place within the UK (7b).

Background notes

This example is typical of the maps which accompany promotional and information brochures. Such maps are often overlooked as a source of information about a place. In addition to giving information, they offer an opportunity to practise the skills of giving and following directions.

Vocabulary

Birmingham, transport, reservation, available, international, timetable, information, alternative, arena, junction, key.

Discussing the text

◆ Focus on the address at the top of the first page. Talk about postcodes with the children and how the country is divided into different regions, each using the first one or two letters of the regional post office in the postcode, for example *B* for Birmingham, *GU* for Guildford.

◆ Talk about the website address and the use of abbreviations, such as *co* for *company*. Ask the children to tell you any other abbreviations that they know of. Do they know what *www* and *http* (Hypertext Transport Protocol) stand for?

◆ Look at the abbreviated labels on the second map, page 120, for example *B'ham* and *Junc*. Can the children suggest what these abbreviations are short for? Why do they think we use abbreviations on maps?

◆ Talk about the layout of the text on both pages. Why do the children think the labels are printed? Do they find them easy to read? Can they suggest any changes or improvements to the layout of the map? (For example, could the roads be shown more simply and more diagrammatically, like the London underground map, to make it easier to read and leave more space for text?)

◆ Talk about the key to the second map. Is it comprehensive? Discuss standard symbols with the children, which are often assumed to be understood, such as the *P* in the square, or the railway station symbol.

◆ Where do the children think they would see a text like this? What sort of people do they think would use a text like this?

Geography activities

◆ Help the children to find Birmingham on a map of the UK. Using the first map and text, discuss the transport links into Birmingham. How well is it served by road, rail and air? Identify the motorways which serve the city. Where can we travel using motorways from Birmingham? What is the furthest point they can reach from the city by motorway? How could they travel from the school to Birmingham?

◆ Use the second map to continue work on finding a route to various places. Start by working through, as an example for the children, how to get to the Paragon Hotel from New Street Station. Discuss it first to make sure they understand the rules of turning right and left, and then ask them to write out the instructions on their own. This can be developed using other places on the map.

◆ Ask the children to write instructions for others to try and follow. Ask them to plan a visit to the Paragon Hotel in Birmingham and to include instructions on how to get there by either car or train.

◆ Get the children to visit the Paragon Hotel website and to cost out a stay there.

◆ Point out that to the east of Birmingham is the National Exhibition Centre (NEC), where many large exhibitions are held, such as the motor show, the boat show and the Clothes Show exhibition. Do the children think it is in a good location? Can they identify all the transport links to the NEC?

◆ Ask the children how they would find out about the NEC using the Internet and encourage them to search for it this way. Then ask them to design a poster to advertise the NEC as a place to hold an exhibition at. They will need to think about location and ease of getting there, the space available, car parking facilities, and so on, and feature these in their posters.

◆ Give the children copies of the Highway Code in order to look at the rules of motorway travel. Who and what cannot use them for instance? What does the letter S stand for on motorway maps? (Services.) What are the speed limits? Ask the children to compose a fact file on motorways, using descriptions, drawings and diagrams to enhance their work.

◆ Show the class a road map of another European country. Find the motorways and look at the links between cities. Do the children know what motorways are called in different countries? (For example, *autobahn* in Germany, *autostrada* in Italy and *autoroute* in France.) Many countries ask travellers to pay a toll for using the motorways. Why do the children think this is? What do the children think about implementing this in Britain? Remind them that it would not only affect personal movement, but transport of food, goods and fuel. Develop a small debate on the pros and cons of introducing toll motorways in Britain.

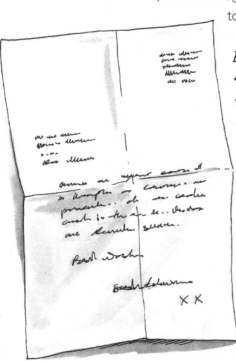

Further literacy ideas

◆ Talk about the setting out of formal letters with the children. In a shared writing lesson, show them how to set out a business letter with the address of the person being written to on the left-hand side of the page. Ask them to practise by writing a letter to the Paragon Hotel to book a room. Remind them that they should include all the information that the hotel will need, the type of room, the date they wish to stay and any other requirements they might have. Make sure they know to organise the letter into paragraphs, too.

◆ Revise the way that instructions are written with the children. Explain that they are usually written in the second person. Ask the children to write a set of instructions for getting from one specified place to another on the map.

◆ Use the part of the text about public transport and tell the children to construct a chart listing all the verbs, such as *follow*, *contact*, *drive*. Then ask them to list the past and future tenses of each of these verbs in the chart. Make a note about any noticeable patterns used to create the past tense, such as adding *-ed*.

◆ The children could design an advertisement for a local tourist attraction or hotel in their area. Make sure they consider the layout of their advertisement and tailor this to their target audience. They may wish to use IT resources to lay out and design their adverts.

The Watercress Line

Genre
information/
persuasive
leaflet

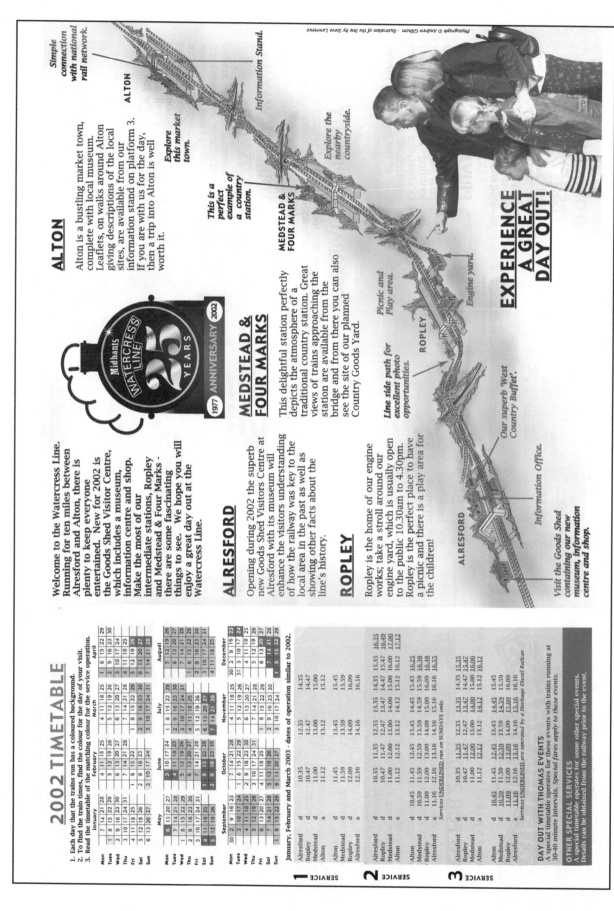

Welcome to the Watercress Line. Running for ten miles between Alresford and Alton, there is plenty to keep everyone entertained. New for 2002 is the Goods Shed Visitor Centre, which includes a museum, information centre and shop. Make the most of our intermediate stations, Ropley and Medstead & Four Marks – there are some fascinating things to see. We hope you will enjoy a great day out at the Watercress Line.

ALTON

Alton is a bustling market town, complete with local museum. Leaflets, on walks around Alton giving descriptions of the local sites, are available from our information stand on platform 3. If you are with us for the day, then a trip into Alton is well worth it.

Simple connection with national rail network.

Information Stand.

Explore this market town.

This is a perfect example of a country station.

MEDSTEAD & FOUR MARKS

This delightful station perfectly depicts the atmosphere of a traditional country station. Great views of trains approaching the station are available from the bridge and from there you can also see the site of our planned Country Goods Yard.

Explore the nearby countryside.

ALRESFORD

Opening during 2002 the superb new Goods Shed Visitors Centre at Alresford with its museum will enhance the visitors understanding of how the railway was key to the local area in the past as well as showing other facts about the line's history.

ROPLEY

Ropley is the home of our engine works; take a stroll around our engine yard, which is usually open to the public 10.30am to 4.30pm. Ropley is the perfect place to have a picnic and there is a play area for the children!

Picnic and Play area.

Engine yard.

Line side path for excellent photo opportunities.

ROPLEY

Our superb 'West Country Buffet'.

ALRESFORD

Information Office.

Visit the Goods Shed containing our new museum, information centre and shop.

EXPERIENCE A GREAT DAY OUT!

Midhants WATERCRESS LINE 25 YEARS — 1977 ANNIVERSARY 2002

Photograph © Andrew Gilham – Illustration of the line by Steve Lawrence

2002 TIMETABLE

1. Each day that the trains run has a coloured background.
2. To find the train times, find the colour for the day of your visit.
3. Read the timetable of the matching colour for the service operation.

[calendar grid Jan–December]

January, February and March 2003 – dates of operation similar to 2002.

SERVICE 1

Alresford	d	10.35	12.35	14.35			
Ropley	d	10.47	12.47	14.47			
Medstead	d	11.00	13.00	15.00			
Alton	a	11.12	13.12	15.12			
Alton	d	11.45	13.45	15.45			
Medstead	d	11.59	13.59	15.59			
Ropley	d	12.09	14.09	16.09			
Alresford	a	12.16	14.16	16.16			

SERVICE 2

Alresford	d	10.35	11.35	12.35	13.35	14.35	15.35	16.35
Ropley	d	10.47	11.47	12.47	13.47	14.47	15.47	16.49
Medstead	d	11.00	12.00	13.00	14.00	15.00	16.00	17.00
Alton	a	11.12	12.12	13.12	14.12	15.12	16.12	17.12
Alton	d	10.45	11.45	12.45	13.45	14.45	15.45	16.25
Medstead	d	10.59	11.59	12.59	13.59	14.59	15.59	16.38
Ropley	d	11.09	12.09	13.09	14.09	15.09	16.09	16.48
Alresford	a	11.16	12.16	13.16	14.16	15.16	16.16	16.55

Services UNDERLINED run on SUNDAYS only.

SERVICE 3

Alresford	d	10.35	11.35	12.35	13.35	14.35	15.35	
Ropley	d	10.47	11.47	12.47	13.47	14.47	15.47	
Medstead	d	11.00	12.00	13.00	14.00	15.00	16.00	
Alton	a	11.12	12.12	13.12	14.12	15.12	16.12	
Alton	d	10.45	11.45	12.45	13.45	14.45	15.45	
Medstead	d	10.59	11.59	12.59	13.59	14.59	15.59	
Ropley	d	11.09	12.09	13.09	14.09	15.09	16.09	
Alresford	a	11.16	12.16	13.16	14.16	15.16	16.16	

Services UNDERLINED are operated by a Heritage Diesel Railcar

DAY OUT WITH THOMAS EVENTS
A special timetable operates for these events with trains running at 30–40 minute intervals. Special fares apply to these events.

OTHER SPECIAL SERVICES
A special timetable operates for some other special events. Details can be obtained from the railway prior to the event.

The Watercress Line

Geography learning objectives

◆ To ask questions, and collect and record evidence (1a, 1b,).

◆ To analyse evidence, draw conclusions, and identify different viewpoints about geographical issues (1c, 1d).

◆ To use atlases, globes and maps, as well as sources of secondary information (2c, 2d).

◆ To explain patterns made by human features in the landscape (4a).

◆ To study at a range of scales (7a).

Background notes

The Watercress Line, operating in mid-Hampshire, is typical of the many small restored railways around the country. The annual brochures for these railways are full of information about the area and the attractions which are on offer throughout the year.

Vocabulary

Passengers, railway, journey, watercress, information, traditional, connections, facilities, services, locomotives, fares, diesel.

Discussing the text

◆ Explain to the children that the text forms a leaflet and ask them to tell you which part they think is the front. How can they tell? What information do the children think the leaflet will include based on this? Make a collaborative list of the ideas suggested on a flip chart.

◆ Discuss the 'Day out with Thomas' section of the text. Who do the children think this is designed to appeal to? How have the leaflet's authors and designers tried to market the attraction?

◆ Discuss the overall layout of the leaflet, looking at the sub-headings. Do the children think the information is well presented? Are the fonts and typesizes appropriate for the information and the audience? Ask the children to highlight the information that they think is the most important – the key words and phrases.

◆ Discuss the information given on the different places, such as Alresford, and Ropley. Which of these would the children like to visit, and what is it about the description that appeals to them?

◆ Look at the 'Special Events 2002' part of the text and talk about any that interest the children, such as the 'War on the line' weekend. How do they think it would feel to pretend to be living during wartime for the day?

Geography activities

◆ Using an atlas or maps of the area, identify the places mentioned in the timetable. A road atlas is particularly suitable for this type of activity. On a base map, ask the children to name the main towns and natural features in southern England.

◆ Use the example of the train timetable in the text to discuss with the children how a timetable is used. Collect together some bus and train timetables from your local area, and after working through some examples give the children some questions to work through themselves, such as *If you need to be in 'x' place by 1pm which train will you need to get? How many stops will it make before your destination?*

The London underground map is also an excellent one to base questions on.

◆ Talk about how the area sells itself by identifying all the interesting points to visit in Alton, Alresford and the other nearby places. Ask the children to draw up a similar list of events and places to visit in their local area in the same format. This can be done in groups and the work displayed. Tell the children to remember to think about the different age groups catered for in their audience and the differing choices their audience might make about what they want to see.

◆ Ask the children to design a poster to go with the text written in the previous activity. Discuss with the class the things that 'sell' an event or place. Ask them to design a poster to promote one of the aspects of the Watercress Line, such as the magical Christmas trips offered. How will they capture the interest of the different age groups pictorially and through the poster's design?

◆ Find out about other railway attractions and working railways. (Severn Railway, North York Moors, Settle–Carlisle, see page 135.) There are also many narrow steam gauge railways over Britain. Ask the children to use the Internet and research books to locate information on these. What do they think is the appeal of such railways? Get them to mark the locations of these other railways on a map. What is the pattern like over the country? What are the modern railway lines called?

Further literacy ideas

◆ Read 'From a railway carriage' by RL Stevenson to the children. Ask them to write a poem or piece of prose commenting in a similar way about what a passenger would see from the train as they travel along the Watercress Line.

◆ Ask the children to identify all the different punctuation used in the text, commas, dashes, colons. Ask the children to label a copy of the text explaining the use of each, for example *A comma is used here to indicate a pause.*

◆ Ask the children to take the 'Thomas' section of the leaflet and rewrite it for younger children, explaining what is offered and using complete sentences.

◆ Look at compound words in the text, such as *Watercress, timetable.* Ask the children to collect as many examples of these as they can.

Read this, or get lost.

Orienteering: The sport with a sense of direction

Genre
procedural
and
information
text within a
publicity
brochure
(with
persuasive
elements)

Orienteering is a fascinating sport using a map and compass to find your way among various check points located across the countryside. An established activity around the world, Orienteering is now gaining popularity in both the United States and Canada.

On an Orienteering course, participants run against the clock to locate pre-established control points through the use of their map and compass navigation skills. The winner is the person best able to read the map and choose a route that leads to the finish line in the shortest time.

Orienteering has been nicknamed "cunning running" because it is the strategist who can use map and compass skills to the best advantage who often wins over a faster runner.

Using a topographical map

A topographical map shows you the lay of the land. Brown contour lines show where hills, valleys and canyons are located. Green and white areas show the location of forests and clearing. Blue depicts lakes, rivers and streams. Black indicates cultural features like backpacking trails and buildings. Other symbols show where ghost towns, abandoned mines, Indian ruins, marshes, swamps, waterfalls, cold springs, hot springs, salt licks, camp sites, coral reefs, beaches, rapids, glaciers, bridges, tunnels, caves and many other exciting features are located. The map legend identifies these symbols. In fact, by looking at a topographical map, you can preplan an entire backpacking, canoeing, hunting trip or camera safari right from your kitchen table!

Use the map to plot the best routes to hike or climb. Locate possible areas for big game or where marshes and swamps attract ducks, geese, waterfowl and other wildlife. Pinpoint portage routes. Pick campsites. Then use the Silva 1-2-3 System with a map to find your way *to* those areas, and find your way *back*!

© Silva Ltd

Direction-finding with the Silva System is as easy as 1-2-3!

Now you're in the woods again, but this time you've brought your Silva compass and a topographical map.

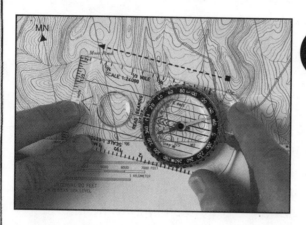

1 Before you start on your way, place the compass on the map with the baseplate edge connecting where you are and where you want to go.

2 Turn the compass dial until the "N" points to magnetic "North" on the map.

3 Hold the compass level in front of you with the direction of travel arrow pointing straight ahead. Turn your body *until the red end of the needle* is directly over the orienting arrow, pointing to the "N" on the dial. The direction of travel arrow now points precisely to your destination. Look up, sight on a landmark and walk to it. Repeat this procedure until you reach your destination.

© Silva Ltd

Where does the North Pole come from?

Actually, there are two North Poles.

The *Magnetic North* is the pole that attracts compass needles. It lies more than 800 miles south of *Geographic North* (also called *True* North), which cartographers show as the top of the world. Because maps are drawn in relation to Geographic North, there is a difference between the compass Magnetic North and the map North. This difference is called *magnetic declination*.

Magnetic declination differs from place to place. So, when the compass is used with a map, the compass reading should be

adjusted accordingly.

With most simple compasses, you must mentally add or subtract the amount of magnetic declination to get an accurate bearing. But with Orienteering compasses like the Silva Ranger, and Explorer Type 1-TD, you can preset the compass dial for magnetic declination and get an accurate reading *automatically*.

How did the compass come to be?

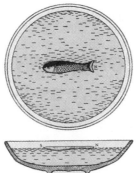

About 2500BC some sage Chinese discovered that when lodestone was placed on a piece of wood floating in water, it always turned to the same direction. From this simple observation, the compass needle was invented – a strip of magnetized steel balanced on a pivot, free to swing in any direction.

Historians claim that the Greeks also knew of lodestone's unique properties. And by 1000 AD seafaring Arabs and Vikings were using a primitive magnetic compass to assist navigating their vessels.

As far as anyone knows, the compass did not enjoy widespread use in Western civilization until about the 13th Century, when it was described in the writings of Alexander Neckam, a Medieval monk.

Today's compass improvements – like Silva's liquid-filled housing and Swedish steel needle mounted on a sapphire jeweled bearing – allow quick, accurate compass readings and reliability unknown to explorers even 100 years ago!

© Silva Ltd

Read this, or get lost

Geography learning objectives
◆ To ask geographical questions and use appropriate geographical vocabulary (1a, 2a).
◆ To use appropriate fieldwork techniques (2b).
◆ To develop decision-making skills (2g).
◆ To recognise how places fit within a wider geographical context (3g).

Background notes
This is a different sort of information and persuasive writing. As well as setting out a variety of reasons why a compass is important in navigation, it also contains some procedural text on using the compass and information about its history.

Vocabulary
Compass, topographical map, magnetic, contour, orienteering, landmark, civilization, explorers, backpacking, glaciers, safari, campsite, recreation.

Discussing the text
◆ Ask the children to consider the title and discuss what they think the text is about. Tell the children that it is about orienteering – does this surprise them? Do they know what this means? Discuss the title in light of this information and explain how it could be read in another way. Talk about the concept of ambiguity and how headlines or titles can often be misleading.
◆ Read the introductory paragraph 'Orienteering'. Discuss with the children why orienteers need to use a compass with a map. What is its function? (Discuss how it tells us which direction north is.) Talk about the nickname the sport has of 'cunning running' and how good compass skills can beat a fast runner.
◆ Read the paragraph entitled 'Where does the North Pole come from?' with the children. This gives background information about the compass and how it works. Talk about the technical vocabulary used and the concepts explained – were the children aware that there are two norths?
◆ Ask the children to read 'How did the compass come to be?' Do the children know what *sage Chinese* means?
◆ Read through the instructions given under the heading 'Direction-finding… '. Do the children think the instructions are clear? What do they think the use of italic signifies?
◆ Have any of the children ever used a compass? When and where did they use it and did they find it easy to use?
◆ Discuss the overall layout of the text, the font and style, the sub-headings used. Ask the children which features of the text they like and ask them to explain why they find particular features appealing.
◆ Talk about the texts in terms of advertising. Is it always obvious that they are actually part of an advertisement leaflet produced by the makers of Silva Compasses? How is this style of advertising different from other adverts the children have come across? (Do adverts usually have instructions on how to use something – think about a vacuum cleaner advert, for example, does it tell us how to clean a house or when the vacuum cleaner was invented?) Do the children think this type of subtle advertising is effective?

Geography activities

◆ Split the class into groups of two or three and give each group a compass. Ask them to follow the instructions in the 'Direction-finding' part of the text, showing how to use a compass. Once they have set the compass, give them practice in using it with a map. Then take the groups outside and repeat this in the school grounds or the local park to give the children practice of setting and following a compass to reach a given direction or object.

◆ Revise the main points of the compass with the children, and then, as appropriate to their experience and capability, give them road atlases or maps and ask them to work out directions to and from a particular place. They can also set challenges for each other. This exercise can be repeated on a world basis, for example *Which country is east of…?* This makes for a fun activity with a learning outcome.

◆ Discuss with the children the usefulness of a compass. Has anyone used one before? How else could they tell the right direction if they were lost in the countryside? (By using the path of the sun, identifying known features or climbing to gain a viewpoint.) How do they find their own way around in their area? Do they only use routes they know? If so, how do they know they are on the right route? How could they find their way to a place unknown to them? (Ask someone or use a map.)

◆ Ask the children to read all the texts very carefully and to use the clues to identify which country they were written for (*swamps* and *Indian ruins* show that they are written for an American audience).

◆ Using the section entitled 'Using a topographical map', ask the children to list all the geographical features mentioned (*swamp*, *glacier*, and so on) and to create a geographical dictionary with an explanation for each feature. They can make a guess as to the meaning of the words in rough and then check them in a dictionary before copying them out in their own.

◆ Set up a small orienteering course around the school grounds or in the local park. This is easy to do and children enjoy looking for clues. It would be helpful to practise left and right directions, and estimations of 100 metres, for example, to give them confidence to start with.

◆ Draw the children's attention to each of the uses of the compass stated in the 'Using a topographical map' piece of text (canoeing, walking, backpacking). Are there any others the children can think of? Ask them to choose areas of the world they might do these activities in, for example backpacking in Australia. Ask them to draw a map of the country and identify its main towns and features. What other things might they do there? Travel brochures will help to provide research material.

Further literacy ideas

◆ Point out to the children that *Silva* is pronounced in the same way as *silver*, but they are spelled differently and have different meanings. Ask the children of other examples of homophones that they can think of, such as *site/sight*. Get them to list these in a chart, giving a definition for each word.

◆ Based on the slogan *Orienteering: The sport with a sense of direction*, ask the children to invent similar slogans for other sports.

◆ Explain to the children that the word *topographical* has the root *graph*, which can be found in other words, such as *biographical* and *geographical*. Can they find any other words which can be made from this root? Use this to look at the meanings of root words, for example *dec* (ten), *aqua* (water).

◆ Discuss with the children how the main heading 'Read this, or get lost' is ambiguous. Ask them to invent other ambiguous headings that could be used for the texts, such as 'The magnetic north'.

◆ Using the 'Direction-finding' text as a model, ask the children to write instructions for how to use a particular piece of equipment, such as a protractor, a thesaurus or a reference book.

◆ The children can design an advert for Silva compasses for a British audience. They should consider who they think would want to buy the compasses and what they would want to know.

Genre
advertisement
and
information
text

For sale

© IKON Imaging

Starter home

Well-presented, turn-of-the-century terrace house offering 2 dble beds, recep., kit./breakfast room, refitted b/room and wc, courtyard-style gdn. GCH, off-rd parking.
Close to shops and town centre.
Would suit first-time buyer.
No chain.
OIRO £95, 000

For sale

Charming family home

Superbly presented detached family home in popular location, comprising entrance hall, sitting room, fully fitted

© IKON Imaging

kitchen, breakfast room, master bed with en suite, 2 further dble beds, office.
GCH thr'out. Dble glazed.
Secluded, mature gardens with delightful views.
Train station ½ mile. Motorway access 1 mile.
Price on application.

For sale

Geography learning objectives

◆ To ask geographical questions, and collect and record evidence (1a, 1b).

◆ To use appropriate geographical vocabulary (2a).

◆ To use secondary sources of information (2d).

◆ To develop decision-making skills (2g).

◆ To recognise and explain patterns of human features (4a).

Vocabulary

Century, terrace, courtyard, reception, detached, popular, location, en suite, secluded, delightful, motorway.

Discussing the text

◆ Show the children the two titles 'Starter home' and 'Charming family home'. What do they think is meant by each title and what would the main characteristics be?

◆ Discuss the price quoted for the first house. Do the children know what *OIRO* is an abbreviation for? Why do the children think the other advertisement says *price on application*?

◆ Read the description of the starter home with the children. What do they understand *turn of the century* to mean? What is *dble* an abbreviation for? Discuss other abbreviations used in the advertisement, such as *GCH, rd*.

◆ *No chain*. Do the children understand this phrase? Discuss the process of buying and selling houses, and explain to the children how a chain may be created and that it is not of a set length.

◆ Discuss the difference between detached and semi-detached. What characteristics do the children think a 'popular' location will have? Discuss the description of the garden as *secluded* and *mature* - why are these terms included?

◆ Why do the children think the train station and motorway are mentioned in the 'Charming family home' advert? Who might be attracted by these amenities?

◆ Discuss the persuasive language used by estate agents to try and encourage people to buy houses. Do the children think that the information given in adverts is always accurate?

Geography activities

◆ Show the children a number of pictures of different types of housing (terraced, semi-detached, bungalows, town houses) and discuss the various characteristics of each. What are the differences between Victorian and modern terraces, for instance? Look at properties for sale in the local paper and read through the sales blurbs. Why are so many of the words shortened?

◆ Go for a class walk in the local area of the school and try to identify examples of the different types of housing. Take pictures of these with a digital camera to download back at school. Then in groups, the children can select the best examples of the different types and make a display labelling the main characteristics.

◆ Using some of the pictures from the previous activity, ask the children to write blurbs for them, with the style of the text as a model. Give them some unusual properties, such as an island hut or a lighthouse, and get them to repeat this exercise. They could also do this for buildings which are

GEOGRAPHICAL SKILLS   **133**

described in their reading books.

◆ Invite an estate agent to come and speak to the children about the process of selling a house from deciding to sell it to the new owners moving in. Discuss with the visitor beforehand the detail and depth that will be appropriate for the class.

◆ Using a map of the local area, identify some of the more popular areas where people like to live. As a class brainstorm a list of ideas why people are attracted to certain places. (Good transport links, proximity to amenities, park areas.) Then ask the children to create a short questionnaire to ask adults a choice of questions from the list. It might be appropriate to ask them to rank six or eight reasons which can then be entered into a database. Discuss the results.

Further literacy ideas

◆ Choose a selection of different styles of houses from a local paper and ask the children to suggest captions for them, such as *Lovely period home*. Provide the children with thesauruses and ask them to suggest one or two descriptions for each house.

◆ Revise vowels and consonants with the children by focusing on the abbreviations used in the text. Ask them to experiment with abbreviating words of their choice, by removing the vowels and then showing their abbreviations to a partner and asking them to guess what the actual words are.

◆ Ask the children to write a story set in an overgrown garden. Encourage them to use evocative language in their description of the garden so that the reader can build up a vivid picture in their minds.

◆ The children can write a diary entry for someone who is moving house. Tell them to write the entry as if they were the person moving in the first person.

◆ Tell the children that they are going to try and sell a house that is actually very run down and in need of work. In a shared writing lesson show the children how to use persuasive language, for example *it has considerable potential*.

◆ Revise letter-writing procedures with the children. Ask them to write a letter to the estate agents enquiring about the price of the 'Charming family home' in the text. Or they could write a reply from the estate agents which points out further benefits of that particular property.

Genre
information text:
timetable and
notes

Train timetable

Table 36
Settle – Carlisle

Mondays to Saturdays

Miles		AN SX	AN SO	AN SO ◇ D	AN SO ◇ E	AN SX ◇	AN ◇ G	AN ◇	AN ◇ A	AN ◇ A	AN ◇	AN
0	Settle	d	07 16		09 49	09 56	09 56	10 45	11 47	13 46	15 46	18 52	20 22
6¼	Horton in Ribblesdale	d	07 24		09 58	10 05	09 58		11 55	13 54	15 54	19 01	20 31
11	Ribblehead	d	07 32		10 06	10 13	10 06		12 03	14 02	16 02	19 09	20a40
17	Dent	d	07 42		10 15	10 22	10 15		12 13	14 12	16 12	19 18	
20½	Garsdale	d	07 47		10 21	10 28	10 21		12 18	14 17	16 17	19 24	
30¼	Kirkby Stephen	d	08 00	07 28	10 33	10 40	10 33	11 22	12 31	14 30	16 30	19 36	
41	Appleby	d	08 12	07 40	10 47	10 54	10 47	11 36	12 44	14 42	16 42	19 49	
52	Langwathby	d	08 26	07 54	11 00	11 07	11 00		12 58	14 56	16 56	20 02	
56¼	Lazonby & Kirkoswald	d	08 32	08 00	11 06	11 13	11 06		13 04	15 02	17 02	20 08	
61¾	Armathwaite	d	08 39	08 07	11 14	11 21	11 14		13 11	15 09	17 09	20 16	
71¾	Carlisle	a	08 56	08 24	11 29	11 40	11 29	12 13	13 28	15 26	17 26	20 33	

Carlisle – Settle

Mondays to Saturdays

Miles		AN SX	AN SO	AN SX	AN SO	AN SX ◇	AN SO	AN ◇ C	AN ◇	AN ◇	AN	AN ◇ C	AN ◇ B	AN
0	Carlisle	d	06 20			07 55	08 58	09 27	11 54	14 26	15 51		16 22	17 55	
10	Armathwaite	d	06 33			08 08	09 11	09 40	12 07	14 39			16 35	18 08	
15½	Lazonby & Kirkoswald	d	06 41			08 16	09 19	09 48	12 15	14 47			16 43	18 16	
19¾	Langwathby	d	06 47			08 22	09 25	09 54	12 21	14 53			16 49	18 22	
30¾	Appleby	d	07 01			08 37	09 39	10 08	12 35	15 08		16 28	17 05	18 36	
41¼	Kirkby Stephen	d	07a16			08 49	09 52	10 21	12 48	15 21		16 41	17 17	18 49	
51¼	Garsdale	d				09 03	10 05	10 34	13 01	15 34			17 31	19 03	
54¾	Dent	d				09 08	10 10	10 39	13 06	15 39			17 36	19 08	
60¾	Ribblehead	d		07 13	07 16	09 17	10 20	10 49	13 16	15 49			17 45	19 20	21 00
65¼	Horton in Ribblesdale	d		07 19	07 22	09 24	10 26	10 55	13 22	15 55			17 52	19 27	21 06
71¾	Settle	d		07 27	07 30	09 32	10 34	11 03	13 30	16 04	17 16		18 01	19 35	21 14

A 19 January to 23 March
B All Mondays to Fridays, also Saturdays until 12 January and from 30 March
C 23 February to 23 March
D Until 12 January and from 30 March
E 13 January to 17 February
G Until 6 January and from 13 March

b Mondays to Fridays
c Saturdays dep 1630
f Saturdays dep 1904
g Change at Doncaster and Leeds

© Railtrack

How to use this timetable

Mileages between stations served (but not those shown for connecting purposes) are shown on the first page of each timetable.

Unique Timetable Number (as shown on the Insert Map and in the Index to Stations).

Stations served.

Catering Information (see inside front cover).

Indicates the Operating Company of the train concerned (see blue pages)

Indicates the days of the week (and in some cases dates) on which the timetable operates

Table 97
Colne, Burnley, Accrington and Blackburn—Preston—Blackpool

Mondays to Saturdays

Principal stations on the route are shown in **bold**.

For non-connecting stations only - indicates that additional services between these stations are included on other timetables (see also below under Route Diagrams).

Indicates the minimum interchange time (in minutes) that should be allowed when connecting between trains. Where no figure is shown, a minimum of 5 minutes should be allowed.

Train runs on Saturdays Only

Seat Reservations symbols (see inside front cover).

Train time in *italics* indicate connecting times. The letter 'a' alongside a connecting station indicates the arrival time at that station. Conversely, the letter 'd' indicates the departure time.

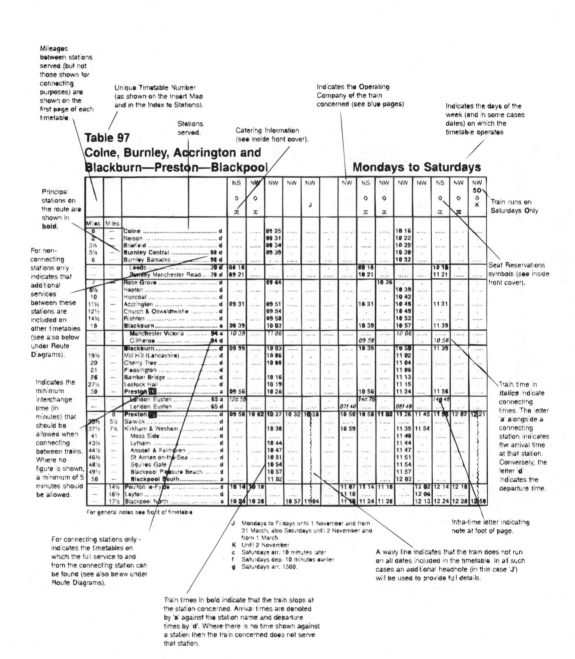

Miles	Miles			NS ◇ ♨	NW ◇ ♨	NW	NW	NW J		NW	NS ◇ ♨	NW	NW	NW	NS ◇ ♨	NW ♨	NW 50 ◇ ♨ K
0	—	Colne	d	.....	.....	09 25	.....	.....		.....	.....	.....	.....	10 16	.....	.....	.....
2	—	Nelson	d	.	.....	09 31	.....	.....		.	.	.....	.....	10 22	.	.	.....
3½	—	Brierfield	d	.	.....	09 34	.....	.....		.	.	.....	.....	10 25	.	.	.....
5½	—	Burnley Central	98 d	.	.....	09 39	.....	.....		.	.	.....	.....	10 30	.	.	.....
6	—	Burnley Barracks	98 d	.	.....	.....	.....	.....		.	.	.....	.....	10 32	.	.	.....
—	—	Leeds	39 d	08 16	.....	.	.	.		09 16	.	.	.	.	10 16	.	.
—	—	Burnley Manchester Road	39 d	09 21	.....	.	.	.		10 21	.	.	.	.	11 21	.	.
7	—	Rose Grove	d	.	.....	09 44	.....	.....		.	10 36	.....	.....	.	.	.	.....
8½	—	Hapton	d	.	.....	.	.	.		.	.	.	.	10 39	.	.	.
10	—	Huncoat	d	.	.....	.	.	.		.	.	.	.	10 42	.	.	.
11½	—	Accrington	d	09 31	.....	09 51	.....	.....		.	10 31	.....	.....	10 46	.	11 31	.....
12½	—	Church & Oswaldtwistle	d	.	.....	09 54	.....	.....		.	.	.....	.....	10 49	.	.	.....
14½	—	Rishton	d	.	.....	09 58	.....	.....		.	.	.....	.....	10 52	.	.	.....
18	—	Blackburn	a	09 39	.....	10 03	.....	.....		.	10 39	.....	.....	10 57	.	11 39	.....
—	—	Manchester Victoria	94 a	10 39	.....	11 06	.	.		.	.	.	.	12 06	.	.	.
—	—	Clitheroe	94 d	.	.....	.	.	.		.	09 58	.	.	.	.	10 58	.
—	—	Blackburn	d	09 39	.....	10 03	.....	.....		.	10 39	.....	.....	10 59	.	11 39	.....
19½	—	Mill Hill (Lancashire)	d	.	.....	10 06	.....	.....		.	.	.....	.....	11 02	.	.	.....
20	—	Cherry Tree	d	.	.....	10 08	.....	.....		.	.	.....	.....	11 04	.	.	.....
21	—	Pleasington	d	.	.....	.	.	.		.	.	.	.	11 06	.	.	.
26	—	Bamber Bridge	d	.	.....	10 16	.....	.....		.	.	.....	.....	11 13	.	.	.....
27½	—	Lostock Hall	d	.	.....	10 19	.....	.....		.	.	.....	.....	11 15	.	.	.....
30	—	Preston	a	09 56	.....	10 26	.....	.....		.	10 56	.....	.....	11 24	.	11 56	.....
—	—	London Euston	65 a	12c 55	.	.	.	.		071 40	.	.	.	.	14g 49	.	.
—	—	London Euston	65 d	.....	.....	.	.	.		.....	14c 76	.	.	081 40	.....	.	.
—	0	Preston	d	09 58	10 02	10 27	10 32	10 38		10 50	10 58	11 02	11 26	11 45	11 56	12 02	12 21
35½	5½	Salwick	d	.....	.....	.	.	.		.....	.....	.....	.....	.	.	.	.
37½	7½	Kirkham & Wesham	d	.	.....	10 36	.....	.....		.	10 59	.....	.....	11 35	11 54	.	.
41	—	Moss Side	d	.....	.....	.	.	.		.....	.....	.....	.....	11 40	.	.	.
43½	—	Lytham	d	.	.....	10 44	.....	.....		.	.	.....	.....	11 44	.	.	.
44½	—	Ansdell & Fairhaven	d	.	.....	10 47	.....	.....		.	.	.....	.....	11 47	.	.	.
46½	—	St Annes-on-the-Sea	d	.	.....	10 51	.....	.....		.	.	.....	.....	11 51	.	.	.
48½	—	Squires Gate	d	.	.....	10 54	.....	.....		.	.	.....	.....	11 54	.	.	.
49½	—	Blackpool Pleasure Beach	d	.	.....	10 57	.....	.....		.	.	.....	.....	11 57	.	.	.
50	—	Blackpool South	a	.	.....	11 02	.....	.....		.	.	.....	.....	12 02	.	.	.
—	14½	Poulton-le-Fylde	d	10 14	10 18	.	.	.		11 07	11 14	11 18	.	12 02	12 14	12 18	.
—	16½	Layton	d	.	.....	.	.	.		11 10	.	.	.	12 06	.	.	.
—	17½	Blackpool North	a	10 24	10 28	.	10 57	11 04		11 18	11 24	11 28	.	12 13	12 24	12 28	12 50

For general notes see front of timetable

For connecting stations only - indicates the timetables on which the full service to and from the connecting station can be found (see also below under Route Diagrams).

Train times in bold indicate that the train stops at the station concerned. Arrival times are denoted by 'a' against the station name and departure times by 'd'. Where there is no time shown against a station then the train concerned does not serve that station.

J Mondays to Fridays until 1 November and from 31 March, also Saturdays until 2 November and from 1 March
K Until 2 November
c Saturdays arr. 10 minutes later
f Saturdays dep. 10 minutes earlier
g Saturdays arr. 1500.

A wavy line indicates that the train does not run on all dates included in the timetable. In all such cases an additional headnote (in this case 'J') will be used to provide full details.

Intra-time letter indicating note at foot of page.

© Railtrack

Train timetable

Geography learning objectives

◆ To collect and record evidence, and draw conclusions (1b, 1c).

◆ To use atlases, maps and secondary sources of information (2c, 2d).

◆ To identify where places are and what they are like (3a–c).

Background notes

This text is designed to provide a challenge, but can be used at a variety of levels, according to the complexity and level of questioning employed.

The Settle–Carlisle railway is a very scenic rail journey of historic and architectural interest, passing through the Yorkshire Dales, the High Pennines and the Eden Valley over many huge viaducts and through long tunnels.

Vocabulary

Timetable, Settle, Carlisle, notice, connecting, information.

Discussing the text

◆ Ask the children to look at the places listed at the top of the timetable, Settle and Carlisle. Do they know where these places are? Have any of the children been on the Settle–Carlisle railway?

◆ Look at the overall text together and ask the children to tell you what it shows. Then talk about timetables in general, and ask what modes of transport use timetables. Where do they think timetables are usually displayed?

◆ Using the 'How to use this timetable' part of the text, ensure that the children understand how to read a timetable and model how to do this, if necessary.

◆ Look with the children at the notes under the timetable. Ask the children to work out how the notes relate to the timetable. Why do the children think that the information is written out in this way? Why do they think that the information is not on the timetable itself?

◆ Why do the children think that there are two timetables with the same places on them? (For outward and return journeys.)

Geography activities

◆ Help the children to find the places mentioned in the timetable on a map of the UK and talk about where they are in relation to the school.

◆ Ask the children to plan a day out for an imaginary visit to some of the places on the timetable. They can use the timetable to work out what time to go and when to come back. Tell them to consult the notes to check if the train they want to take is running. Pose questions, such as *If you were to miss your train how long would you have to wait for the next one?* This is an excellent opportunity for the children to use the 24-hour clock in a practical and useful way.

◆ Show the children pictures of viaducts. (The Settle-Carlisle Railway Development Company has a useful website at www.settle-carlisle.co.uk which provides interesting facts and pictures of the railway.) Why do they think they were built? (To cross valleys.) The children could draw their own pictures of viaducts for display in the classroom.

◆ Carlisle is the last English town on the west-coast mainline train route into Scotland. Use a map of Great Britain with the class to identify other border towns and villages between England and Scotland, then do the same for the border towns on the east-coast mainline route to Scotland from London. Explain to the children that 400 years ago Carlisle was a true border town but that today travel is possible freely over the border. Give an example of a true border town, such as Basle in Switzerland, and discuss how some European countries have full border controls (this also gives an opportunity to explore aspects of the EU with the children).

◆ Collect some of the timetables in use in your local area (bus, train, post bus, local airflights). Ask the children to plan journeys to local places using real times and availability as shown on the timetables. Then ask them to compare the relative times and costs of different types of travel to the same place. Use a suitable map of the area as the basis for a wall display and ask the children to summarise their journey details in a standard format, for example *From/To/Day of week/Time taken/Cost* and add these to the display so that comparison can be made easily.

Further literacy ideas

◆ Use the place names in the text as a starting point for revising proper nouns. Then give the children a list of words which include some uncapitalised proper nouns and ask them to put in capital letters where needed.

◆ Ask the children to highlight any words they can find in the text that are abbreviated (*arr* and *dep* in the notes). Using local timetables, ask the children to make a list of abbreviations and their meanings, placing them in alphabetical order. Make a class list for display and extend the list as new examples are found.

◆ Get the children to look up *viaduct* in an etymological dictionary. What are its origins? (From Latin, *via* for road and *duct* meaning *to lead, convey*.) What word is it like? (*Aqueduct*.) Can they work out what an aqueduct might do?

◆ Ask the children to find as many compound words in the 'How to use this timetable' text as they can, such as *Blackpool, Blackburn*.

◆ Ask the children to write a story about a train journey. What do they see out of the window of the train? They should include some of the place names from the timetable in the text.

Geographical dictionary

Climate	weather measured over a long period of time
Coast	where the land meets the sea
Deposit	drop, or leave behind
Desert	a land area with less than 250mm of rainfall a year
Environment	the surroundings of a place
Erode	wear away
Flood	an excess of water in the wrong place
Human	linked to people
Marine	connected with the sea
Mountain	upland that is higher and steeper than a hill
Physical	natural landscape
Polar	cold conditions found at the North and South Poles
Rainforest	dense forest in hot rainy areas of the world
River	a large natural stream of water flowing to the sea
Stream	small, often fast-flowing, river
Transport	carry, or move to another place
Tropical	very hot, humid conditions
Valley	a dip or trough in the landscape
Village	a small settlement

Geographical dictionary

Geography learning objectives

◆ To ask geographical questions, and collect and record evidence (1a, 1b).

◆ To use appropriate geographical vocabulary (2a).

◆ To use secondary sources of information (2d).

◆ To recognise and explain a variety of both physical and human features (4a, 4b).

Vocabulary

Dictionary, upland, surrounding, excess, landscape, humid, variety, services, reference, information.

Discussing the text

◆ Discuss with the children what a geographical dictionary is. What sort of words do the children think such a dictionary might contain? Can the children suggest any other subject-specific dictionaries that they have come across – or that they think might be available, such as a scientific or mathematical one?

◆ Take each of the words in turn from the list and discuss them with the children. Check their pronunciation. You could place the text on an OHP first and ask the children to predict what some of the words mean before revealing the definition.

◆ Discuss some of the definitions listed for the words. Could the children suggest any other ways of defining the words?

◆ Look at the list of words. Are they in any particular order? How else could they be ordered?

◆ Can the children think of any other reference books they may encounter? Ask them to think more widely, for example what might a doctor or a car mechanic use to consult for information?

Geography activities

◆ Before giving the children the text, read out the geography words only and ask them to write down their own definitions of them. Then ask them to compare their definitions with the explanations in the text. They can also look up the words in another dictionary and compare all three to see the similarities and differences. Discuss the difficulties of making an explanation straightforward enough to explain the meaning clearly, and yet remaining simple at the same time.

◆ Ask the children to make a list of the words down one side of a piece of paper and to draw two sets of boxes alongside each word. In the first box ask them to create a clear but interesting symbol

GEOGRAPHICAL SKILLS

to represent the word, perhaps one they could use on a map. In the second box, ask them to find the actual symbol on an OS map and draw it in. Which words have they not been able to find represented or to draw as symbols?

◆ On a very large sheet of paper, or on the classroom wall, ask the children to create an imaginary landscape and to draw in features for as many of the words in the text as they can. Can they make the picture a continuous and realistic representation? Get them to label the features. This can be done as an exercise for large or small groups, and should involve discussions about layout, design, representation and creativity.

◆ Ask the children to create a similar dictionary for their local area. Tell them to discuss all the words which identify or describe the area, and create a similar list to the one in the text but with a specific focus.

◆ Discuss with the children how easy it is to define the differences between a stream and a river, for example, or to decide what a town is – when does a village stop being a village and become a town? Explain that this is to do with the amount of service provision as well as the population. There can be large villages with only a few shops, but a small town, no larger than the village, with lots of shops, and that this varies around the country. Ask the class to conduct a small survey amongst adults to find out what they think the definitions mean, and to discuss their findings.

Further literacy ideas

◆ Ask the children to put some of the words into sentences, for example *A place with a variety of shops and services is called a town*. Use this as an opportunity to revise capital letters and full stops.

◆ Look at the words that have the suffix *-al* added to them with the children, for example *tropic-al*, *geographic-al*. Use these examples to discuss how nouns can become adjectives and ask the children to find other examples of adjectives that have been, or could be, created in this way, in the text and maybe in their reading books.

◆ Give the children some words from the text and ask them to look them up in a dictionary. Ask them to focus on the further information that is given, such as their origins, multiple meanings and grammatical category. Point out how the grammatical categories are different according to what suffix the words take.

◆ In a guided reading session, the children can practise segmenting words into phonemes for reading and spelling purposes, for example *moun-tain*, *en-vi-ron-ment-al*. Use some of the words in individual spelling lists.

◆ Choose one of the features listed in the text, such as a rainforest or a desert, and ask the children to develop a story set in one of these places. Encourage them to use descriptive vocabulary to build up a picture of the setting.

Make a visitor's guide

Your guide to the local area should contain:

● Text, pictures and a simple 'how to get there' map.
● An exciting design so that people want to read it.
● Plenty of information, that is well set out and easy to read.

Use both sides of a piece of A4 paper and fold in three:

How to make a local guide for your area:

1. ● Brainstorm all the places locally that people might like to visit.
● Find out about leisure activities in your area.
● Collect local books and papers that might give you more information.
● Check the information in your local library.

2. ● Decide which information should go in the guide.
● Decide on any maps or illustrations you wish to use.

3. Design your guide; make it eye-catching as well as informative.

4. Produce it on the computer.

Make a visitor's guide

Geography learning objectives

◆ To ask geographical questions (1a).

◆ To collect and record evidence (1b).

◆ To analyse evidence and draw conclusions (1c).

◆ To communicate in ways appropriate to the task and the audience (1e).

◆ To carry out fieldwork investigations (7c).

Background notes

Although the text stands as an instructional guide in its own right, it also presents a clear brief to help the children make a tourist leaflet about their own, or a neighbouring area. It also aids children in working out how to phrase useful questions, a skill which can be employed in future questionnaires and fieldwork.

Vocabulary

Guide, attractions, information, library, illustrations, leisure, mention, brainstorm.

Discussing the text

◆ Discuss the title of the text with the class. What would the children expect to find in a visitor's guide to an area? Make a list of the children's ideas on a flip chart.

◆ Discuss the phrase *How to make a local guide for your area*. How would the children describe this sentence – is it a statement or a question? Discuss with them what an instruction is and the sort of words that are used in instructions, for example *make, produce*. Brainstorm a list of words together that could be used in instructions.

◆ Look at the instructions listed in the text with the children. Focus on the language used and ask them to underline the key words. Then ask them to point out any similarities between the words they have underlined.

◆ The text specifies what format the guide should take. Discuss this format with the children – what are its advantages and disadvantages? Can they think of any other information that might be required when following the instructions? Should there be a list of materials or equipment, for example?

◆ Discuss the layout of the instructions with the class. Why are they bullet pointed? What is the advantage of this over writing full sentences?

◆ How will the diagram of the guide help the reader?

Geography activities

◆ Discuss with the children the possibility of producing their own guide for visitors to their area. Talk about what these visitors might like to visit, see or experience. Help them to work out where they would go to find information to put into the guide. Who will they ask? Even if the area is not one that tourists might naturally be drawn to, most areas usually have examples of different types of houses or features which can be used.

◆ Ask the children to work in pairs and, using the information from the previous activity, ask them to follow through the instructions in the text. They will need to think about the illustrations needed for the guide – what form will they take? (Drawings, photographs? Point out that if pictures are taken with a digital camera they can be downloaded and reduced in size.) One of the greatest problems the children are likely to find is choosing from the amount of information they amass! Learning to select will then become a valuable skill.

◆ The class can be taken on a visit to their locality to discuss what might be suitable to include in a guide. They will need to think about access and safety if they are hoping to include specific places. Pose questions to them, such as *Will visitors be able to walk around the features? How will they travel between sites? If transport is used, are there parking facilities available? What about toilets?*

◆ Carry out a class survey to find out what people look for when they visit places. Creating this survey will provide an opportunity to look at how questions should be presented in a questionnaires. Discuss the use of *Where? Why? What?* and *When?* This will help the children recognise how much more information these words trigger rather than the question *Do you…?* Talk about the layout of a questionnaire and the usefulness of multiple-choice questions that produce easily accessible data. The children should experiment first with a pilot questionnaire to test out the usefulness of the questions on a couple of people. Finally, when the information from the real questionnaires has been collected, create a database so that the answers can be fed in quickly in readiness for analysis.

◆ Find some brochures which give examples of places that have been developed into visitor centres, such as coalmines or old industrial complexes. Can the children suggest what these places were used for? How important would they have been in the local area? (For example, would they have been a big employer? What would have happened to the workers when the places closed?) Finally, discuss what sort of jobs these developments can bring to a community.

Further literacy ideas

◆ Discuss the features of instructional writing with the children, for example verbs placed at the beginning of sentences and in the imperative form, a specific ordering of sentences, such as chronologically, and so on.

◆ Make a class list of all the verbs used as a command in the text, such as *find, decide, produce*. Then get the children to put each of these into a sentence of their own.

◆ Ask the children to write down a list of all the verbs they can find in the text. Then ask them to identify the past, present and future tense of each verb they have listed. Ask them to make a note of similarities in the spelling of the different versions of the words and of any exceptions.

◆ Give the children a list of statements based on the text and ask them to write down whether they are true or false, such as *The leaflet should be folded into three sections.*

◆ Ask the children to draw a flow chart to represent the instructions.

◆ Give the children the instructions in a mixed-up order. Ask them to sequence the instructions correctly.

◆ Give the children a writing frame to help them write simple instructions, for example *You will need…, first…, then…, when…* Then ask the children to write simple instructions for an everyday activity, such as following a simple recipe.

◆ Give the children a piece of prose and ask them to rewrite the information in a bullet-pointed list format.

◆ Get the children to make nouns from verbs using words from the text, for example *produce/production, decide/decision*.